VNAF
South Vietnamese Air Force
1945-1975

By Jim Mesko

Illustrated by Don Greer

TO-QUỐC KHÔNG GIAN

squadron/signal publications, inc.

An A-1H Skyraider of the 514th Fighter Squadron, 23rd Tactical Wing during 1966.

Authors Note:

The Vietnamese Air Force (VNAF) existed for only twenty-four years, from the summer of 1951, when the French began training Vietnamese aircrews, until the spring of 1975 — when Saigon fell. When the end came most, if not all, official records were either destroyed or captured by the communists and it is unlikely that the complete story of the Vietnamese Air Force will ever be told, to the regret of anyone interested in the history of the war in Southeast Asia.

In *VNAF 1945-1975* I have tried to trace the history of the Vietnamese Air Force from its inception under the French, through the final days of the South Vietnamese collapse. The account that follows is based on official U.S. government publications, interviews with Vietnamese pilots, interviews with American pilots who were closely associated with the VNAF, and personal observations and notes made while I was assigned to an American-Vietnamese advisory team based near Tan Son Nhut during 1971 and 1972.

The photographs have come from both official and private sources and were chosen to present as complete a coverage as possible of the great variety of aircraft used by the VNAF. Unfortunately there are gaps in this coverage, notably in both the early period under the French, and during the final days when Vietnam finally succumbed to the communists. While there were supposedly a large number of official U.S. photos taken during the final days just before the communist takeover — and afterwards, when some of the former Vietnamese aircraft were returned to the United States, I have been able to locate few photographs dealing with these time frames, even with the help of Defense Department researchers. Perhaps some day these photos will surface and add additional information to the history of the Vietnamese Air Force, but until such time as this occurs the last few months of the VNAF will remain obscure.

On a number of occasions during preparation of this book I was forced to pass judgment on conflicting pieces of information. When such situations arose I consulted a number of knowledgeable people before making a final determination of either the accuracy or authenticity of the information. And, while these people proved extremely helpful, the final decision was mine and I must take full responsibility for any errors which may have occurred. I encourage anyone who has additional information or photographs on the VNAF to contact me, so that eventually the fullest and most complete record of the South Vietnamese Air Force can be told.

Jim Mesko
Akron, Ohio 1987

ISBN 0-89747-193-8

If you have any photographs of the aircraft, armor, soldiers or ships of any nation, particularly wartime snapshots, why not share them with us and help make Squadron/Signal's books all the more interesting and complete in the future. Any photograph sent to us will be copied and the original returned. The donor will be fully credited for any photos used. Please send them to:

Squadron/Signal Publications, Inc.,
1115 Crowley Drive
Carrollton, TX 75011-5010.

Dedication

This book is dedicated to all those who fought and died in the skies over Vietnam for the cause of freedom.

In Memory

To the memory of Rusty whose tragic and needless death left a void in the lives of those who knew and loved him.

Photo Credits and Assistance

Colonel Knox Bishop
Wayne Mutza
Ray Leader, Flightleader
Tom Hansen
Pham Quang Khiem
Bob Steinbrunn
USAF
French Air Force
USAF Museum
USAF Books & Magazine Branch
Dana Bell
Joe Michaels, JEM Aviation
Bob Chenoweth
Dave Menard
Steve Daniels
Nicholas J. Waters III
US Army
ECPA/SHAA
Defense Audio Visual Agency
IPMS USA

I would like to thank the following people who helped make this book possible; Stella Mesko who proofread and typed the manuscript, Faith Andrus who served as my official translator for the French 'Connection', Bob Mills who helped sort out numerous bits of contradictory information, Pham Quang Khiem who provided valuable material on the VNAF organization, and Pat, my lovely wife, who lived with this book for far longer then she should have.

Introduction

During the spring of 1975, the United States supported government of Nguyen Van Thieu quickly succumbed to a massive offensive by the North Vietnamese Army (NVA). One of the key reasons for the rapid collapse of South Vietnam was the inability of the South Vietnamese Air Force (VNAF) to provide adequate air support to the Army of the Republic of Vietnam (ARVN). This failure was due to a rapidly changing and increasingly hostile air environment for which the VNAF was ill equipped and unprepared.

As part of its early preparations for their thrust southward, the North Vietnamese Army (NVA) had moved in large numbers of radar-controlled Anti-Aircraft Artillery (AAA) pieces and shoulder-launched SA-7 Surface-to-Air Missiles. When the NVA launched its attack, these new air defenses severely limited the VNAF's effectiveness against the rapidly advancing NVA.

Just three years earlier, during the Easter Invasion of 1972, the Army of the Republic of Vietnam (ARVN) had withstood a similar NVA offensive — but only with the aid of massive American air support. Following this blunted invasion, the U.S. renewed its bombing of North Vietnamese targets while pressuring the North Vietnamese to negotiate an end to the war. In January of 1973 an agreement was finally reached which resulted in the Paris Peace Accords, supposedly ending the Vietnam War. Under the terms of this agreement, the United States began to withdraw its forces from South Vietnam. Prior to the final withdrawal the United States began a massive air and sea lift of supplies and equipment to insure that the South Vietnamese would have the necessary resources to defend themselves against any renewed onslaught from the North.

The VNAF, under the Enhance Plus program, received large quantities of new equipment, both to replace losses suffered during the 1972 Invasion and to further re-enforce the VNAF so it could assume roles formerly filled by the departing U.S. air forces. On paper, at least, the VNAF was a modern, well rounded force which *theoretically* should have been able to counter any future North Vietnamese attack. Especially since the North Vietnamese Air Force (NVAF) was predominately an air defense force, unable to effectively support the NVA in offensive operations in South Vietnam. Nevertheless, in the years between the signing of the peace accords and the final NVA assault, the VNAF lost the capability to provide support for its army and to interdict NVA supply lines, in the face of an increasingly effective NVA air defense system. The VNAF was virtually helpless in halting the advancing communist armies. Ironically, air support and interdiction had been considered one of the cornerstones for the defense of South Vietnam.

In any examination of the VNAF, it is understandable to try to compare it to the U.S. Air Force after which it had been modeled. On the surface the two organizations may appear somewhat similar, however, in reality the two services were similar only in terms of equipment and to a lesser degree, organization. The strength and effectiveness of any military force rests with its training and *esprit de Corps* of the individuals that make it work, rather than its equipment and weapons. The effectiveness of the North Vietnamese Army time and again proved that the aggressiveness of its troops could overcome the lack of proper equipment and weapons.

While in no way discrediting American pilots, it also must be remembered that American pilots flew a specific number of missions or spent a specific time period 'in-country' and were then rotated out of the combat zone. The VNAF pilot had no such luxury. He would often fly thousands of combat sorties with little respite ... respite which often came in the form of being wounded or killed. This basic difference between the two services must be considered when making a judgment of the VNAF's performance. Unfortunately, the stress of continuous combat on VNAF pilots is often overlooked. The VNAF pilot amassing thousands of combat hours over a five or ten year flying career developed a rather fatalistic view of his chances for survival. By USAF standards the VNAF pilot became cautious ... somewhat similar to an American pilot flying his final missions before rotating home.

In tracing the history of the VNAF, material has been included related to the French Air Force in Indo-China and two U.S. Air Force units which had close ties with the Vietnamese Air Force. In the case of the French, there has been little information on this aspect of the air war in Southeast Asia previously available to the American reader. Since the French were instrumental in the initial formation of the VNAF, this section helps lay the groundwork for the VNAF's early development under French tutelage. In the case of the American units, their direct or indirect association with the VNAF during the first serious expansion of the VNAF during the early 1960s, played a significant role in the VNAF's transition from a small internal security force to the modern, well-equipped air force that eventually developed in the late 1960s.

Over a decade has past since the last sorties were flown by the South Vietnamese Air Force. Some of its aircraft were flown out of the country and were either returned to the United States or turned over to American allies within the region. The remainder were either destroyed or captured by the victorious North Vietnamese. A number of these were used by the North Vietnamese to form additional squadrons to supplement their own small air force, particularly in the ground support role.

For the men who made up the VNAF, a similar fate awaited them. Most were captured by the communists and, in some cases, put through re-education camps. Others were pressed into service to maintain or fly the U.S. aircraft left behind. A lucky few were able to escape from South Vietnam and start new lives in the United States, where today they have become part of the American melting pot. Yet on occasion, when these veterans glance at an aircraft high overhead, their thoughts turn to a time when they flew through the skies over South Vietnam in lumbering C-47s, powerful Skyraiders, or sleek F-5s, and they remember long forgotten comrades who made the ultimate sacrifice for freedom. They remember, and for the briefest of moments the VNAF once more exists.

Armee de l'Air (French Air Force)

When Japan surrendered in August of 1945, the Allies, under the terms of the Potsdam Agreement, deployed British and Chinese troops to Indo-China to oversee the disarmament of the Japanese forces in the region. These Allied troops were to remain until sufficient French forces were available to relieve them. The country was divided into two zones of occupation, with the British being assigned to the southern sector (below the 16th parallel) and the Chinese being responsible for the north. The Viet Minh, a Vietnamese communist dominated guerrilla group led by Ho Chi Minh, began making a bid for political control of the French colony and occupied key positions throughout the country. In the south, when the British attempted to maintain control and restore order, clashes erupted between the Viet Minh and British forces. In response, the British armed former French POWs and re-armed some Japanese units to in an effort to drive the Viet Minh from the south.

In the north, the Chinese made little effort to control the activities of the Viet Minh and Ho Chi Minh gradually established control over significant areas of what would eventually become North Vietnam. On 2 September 1945, even before Allied forces had arrived, Ho Chi Minh had declared independence for the Democratic Republic of Vietnam (DRV) with Hanoi as its capital. By late 1945, a compromise agreement had been reached where British and Chinese troops would be replaced by French forces but the Viet Minh would be allowed to retain a degree of autonomy in the areas it controlled.

The first contingent of 150 French troops were ferried into Tan Son Nhut Airport (near Saigon), during September of 1945 by six C-47s of the *Groupe de Marche d'Extreme Orient* (Far East Task Force) and in December of 1945, under the terms of the compromise agreement, French troops entered Hanoi. The French had begun their effort to re-establish colonial rule over Indo-China.

During their early preparations to re-establish an *Armee de l'Air* presence in Indochina, French authorities had taken into consideration American reluctance to see former colonial rulers re-establish dominion over their former possessions. To circumvent any possible U.S. embargo of spare parts for its American-made combat aircraft, the composition of the first *Armee de l'Air* units deployed to Indochina consisted of British and French-made aircraft with the exception of the Douglas C-47. By November of 1945, a contingent of eighteen C-47 transports were in place at Tan Son Nhut and civilian airliners began carrying out regular commercial flights between the *colony* and Metropolitan France.

The first *Armee de l'Air* combat unit to deploy to Vietnam was *Groupe de Chasse* 7 (7th Fighter Group) which was transferred to Tan Son Nhut in December of 1945 — but arrived without its complement of Supermarine Spitfire Mk 9s. Fortunately, 273 Squadron of the Royal Air Force was being withdrawn from the area and loaned twelve Spitfire Mk 8 fighters to *Group de Chasse* 7. The Spitfires were supplemented by some twelve Nakajima Ki 43 IIb and Ki 43 III

Oscar fighters confiscated from the Japanese Army Air Force. These fighters were used to equip the two squadrons within GC 7 (GC I/7 *Province* Ki 43s and GC II/7 *Nice* Spitfires Mk 8s), pending the arrival of their own fighters. In addition, a number of Nakajima A6M2-N Rufe and Aichi E13A Jake float planes (captured from a Japanese cruiser squadron) were acquired from the Allied Technical Air Intelligence Center in Singapore and pressed into service with *Escadrille* 8S of the *Aeronavale* (French Naval Air Arm).

When the uneasy truce between the French and Viet Minh broke down during December of 1945, the Spitfires of GC II/7, operating from Tan Son Nhut, flew the first French combat missions being shortly joined by Ki 43s from GC I/7 flying close support missions from Phon-Penh (Cambodia). A cease fire was eventually worked out and signed on 6 March 1946. As part of the agreement, the French recognized Ho Chi Minh's Democratic Republic of Vietnam as a free state within the Indo-chinese Federation of the French Union. At the same time the French established South Vietnam as an independent republic under the title Chochin China.

Both sides took advantage of the truce to strengthen their forces. GC 7's Spitfire Mk 9s finally arrived and immediately replaced the remaining Ki 43 Oscars assigned to GC I/7. The Oscars had been kept operational with a mixture of hard work, luck and the talents of French salvage teams assisted by Japanese POWs. The only spare parts available for the Oscars had been gathered from salvaged wrecks found in Japanese boneyards scattered throughout South East Asia. To support French Union forces around Hanoi, a number of GC II/7s Spitfires were transferred north, with detachments being assigned to both Gia Lom and Bach Mai airfields on the outskirts of Hanoi.

Further reinforcements arrived from France to supplement the C-47s of the transport unit. Sixteen ACC.1 *Toucans* (French-built Junkers Ju 52 transports) of *Groupe de Transport* I/34 arrived during February of 1946 and were stationed at Bien Hoa airfield northeast of Saigon. The ACC.1 *Toucans* (as had their earlier German counterparts) were pressed into service as level bombers, carrying bombs mounted under the wings and fuselage. Both C-47s and ACC.1s also carried field manufactured napalm canisters in their cargo holds. The napalm canisters were pushed out of the transports' side cargo door, hopefully landing on a target.

A number of Morane-Sauliner MS 500 *Criquet* (French-built versions of the German Fieseler Fi 156C-7 Storch) were supplied for use in the liaison and observation roles by four *Groupes d'Aviation d'Observation d'Artillerie*. The MS 500 *Criquet* was well suited to the rough grass fields used at forward outposts and was extensively used to coordinate air support, evacuate wounded, and transport high ranking officers. Supplementing the MS 500s were a number of Stinson L-5s, Nord Center NC 701 *Martinets* (based on the German Siebel Si 204), and Nord 1001/1002 *Pingouins* (based on the Messerschmitt Bf 108 *Taifun*) used primarily in the liaison role.

A pair of Spitfire LF MK 9s from GC I/4 over the Vietnamese coast near Nha Trang during 1947. During the early years of the war the Spitfire was the only fighter the *Armee de l'Air* had available for use in Indochina. These Spitfires are armed with 250 pound bombs on under wing racks. (ECPA/SHAA)

To effectively use these reinforcements the *Armee de l'Air* reorganized into two separate tactical groups; TFIN in northern Vietnam (Tonkin and northern Amman) and TFIS in southern Vietnam (Cochin-China and southern Amman). Later in the war (1950) this structure would again be reorganized into three groups; *Groupement Aerien Tactique* (Tactical Air Group - GATAC) GATAC North (Tonkin), GATAC Central (Amman) and GATAC South (Cochin-China).

During July 1946 the C-47 transport unit at Tan Son Nhut was designated, *Groupe de Transport* II/15 *Anjou* (although a year later it would be redesignated GT II/64). During August, GC 7 was recalled for occupation duty in Germany and replaced by *Groupe de Chasse* 2. GC 2's squadrons, I/2 *Cigognes* and GC II/2 *Alsace* inherited the Spitfires left behind by the departing GC 7.

On 20 November 1946 an incident between French and Viet Minh troops over who would control the Customs House in Haiphong (and thereby control the flow of arms into Vietnam) erupted into violence. The fighting slowly spread throughout the city and on 23 November, French navy ships began a bombardment to cover the landings of additional French troops. By early December the fighting had spread to Hanoi where Viet Minh troops launched a surprise attack on French forces. On 20 December, Ho broadcast a call for *a war of national resistance*, marking the beginning of full scale war, a war that would last twenty-nine years.

Armee de l'Air Spitfires, ACC.1s and C-47s were able to provide vital air support to French ground units during the first critical days of the Viet Minh surprise attack in Hanoi. With this air support, the Viet Minh was driven from the city in early January and Ho Chi Minh fled to his base camp in the mountains of northern Tonkin. Despite this initial French victory, the Viet Minh guerrillas launched numerous attacks on French outposts, convoys, and even major installations. Hard pressed to meet all the requests for air support, the *Armee de l'Air* urgently requested reinforcements. Additional Spitfires, AAC.1s and C-47s were quickly delivered from France to replace losses and increase unit strength and an additional fighter group was dispatched to Indo-China. GC III/11 *Corse* equipped with de Havilland Mosquito FB Mk 6s was deployed from Rabat, Morocco arriving in February of 1947 at Tan Son Nhut. The Mosquito provided the French with a much needed heavily armed fighter-bomber,

During the late 1940s AAC.1 *Toucan* (French built Junkers Ju 52 transports) were the backbone of the French transport and bomber force in Indochina. These *Toucans*, of GT I/34 (later I/64) *Bearn* line the runway at Tan Son Nhut airfield near Saigon. The designation ACC.1 is carried on the rudder in Black and the Red cross on the third aircraft in line denotes its use in the casualty evacuation role. (USAF)

but its use would be short lived. The humid tropical conditions adversely affected the 'Mossies' wooden structure which began to rapidly deteriorate. Additionally, the Mosquitoes could only be operated from Tan Son Nhut's long runways and after serving only seven months the survivors were withdrawn from service and replaced with Spitfires. A replacement Spitfire fighter group GC 4, made up of GC I/4 *Dauphine* and GC II/4 *La Fayette*, was transferred from France to replace GC 2 which relinquished their Spitfires to the new group and was decommissioned.

In October of 1947 the French launched their first large scale assault on the Viet Minh, *OPERATION LEA*, a combined airborne and ground assault against the main Viet Minh headquarters in northern Tonkin. Supported by *Armee de l'Air* AAC.1s, C-47s and Spitfires, French paratroops, tanks, and infantry stabbed deep into

To direct airstrikes the French used the MS 500 *Criquet*, a French built version of the German Fieseler Fi 156 *Storch*. The Viet Minh developed a healthy respect for French airpower and became masters in the art of camouflage, even in such open terrain as the flat delta regions around Hanoi and Saigon.

A Mosquito FB 6 of GC III/11 *Corse* which operated the Mosquito until tropical conditions began to deteriorate its wooden structure. GC III/11 gradually replaced the Mosquetos first with Spitfires and later (after being renumbered GC I/6) with Bell P-63 Kingcobras. (ECPA/SHAA)

A Spitfire Mk 9, believed to be from GC II/4, on patrol over the Red River Delta near the important northern cities of Hanoi and Haiphong. GC II/4 Spitfires were based at both Gia Lam and Bach Mai airfields near Hanoi. During late 1949 the Spitfires were gradually replaced by Bell P-63C Kingcobras. (ECPA/SHAA)

Viet Minh controlled territory hoping to capture Ho Chi Minh, General Giap, and their respective staffs. Although the attack did achieve some success, Ho and his top advisors evaded capture. With this failure the French lost their one chance to end the war with a single decisive action. There would never be another opportunity to capture the entire Viet Minh hierarchy at one time. Following the *LEA* offensive, the war bogged down with the French controlling the cities and the Viet Minh in control of the countryside. The French were unable to corner the elusive guerrillas in a set battle and the Viet Minh were not strong enough to push the French out of Indochina.

The French had long realized that the Spitfire was ill suited to an air-to-ground war and would have to be replaced. The Spitfire lacked the range to cover distant outposts and its bomb load of normally two 250 or 500 pound bombs was too small for effective ground support. When the Communist takeover of China seemed a certainty, American attitude toward the French in Indochina changed considerably. For the *Armee de l'Air*, this change meant that deployment of American-made aircraft could now be undertaken without fear of embargoes. Originally, the French considered sending Republic P-47D Thunderbolt fighters to Indochina, but these aircraft were needed in France, where they made up the majority of NATO committed fighter-bomber units. It was decided therefore to utilize Bell P-63C Kingcobra fighters to replace the Spitfires.

The first, of what would eventually be over a hundred, P-63C Kingcobras were delivered aboard the French aircraft carrier *DIX-IMUNDE* (formerly HMS BITER) for use by GC I/5 *Vendee* and GC II/5 *Ile de France* during July of 1949. These P-63Cs were survivors of over 300 Kingcobras supplied to France by the United States under lend-lease during the latter part of the Second World War. This first Kingcobra group was quickly followed by three additional groups, GC II/6 *Normendie Niemen*, GC III/6 *Roussillon*, and GC I/9 *Limousin*. The P-63 was more heavily armed than the Spitfire and better suited to the ground support role, tremendously improving the air force's capability to carry out air strikes on communist forces. Additionally, the P-63 was able to survive far more battle damage then the Spitfire, which was particularly important since the Viet Minh had been steadily improving their anti-aircraft capabilities, adding newer and heavier weapons. This fact was dramatically driven home when a P-63C of GC II/5 was shot down by automatic weapons fire on 19 January 1950.

A lineup of Kingcobras, believed to be of GC I/5 *Vendee* on the ramp at Gia Lam between missions. The French deployed over one hundred Bell P-63C Kingcobras to Vietnam during late 1949 as replacements for their war-weary Spitfires. The heavy gunpowder stains on the nose are from the two nose mounted .50 caliber machine guns. (ECPA/SHAA)

A P-63C of GC I/5 *Vendee* being refueled prior to a sortie against the Viet Minh at Lang Son during General Giap's first offensive in the fall of 1950. Despite initial gains the communists were eventually driven back by the French Army, with the aid of air support by *Armee de l'Air* fighter-bombers. (ECPA/SHAA)

The *Armee de l'Air*, fighters along with *Aeronavale* PBY Catalinas, flew coastal surveillance patrols to prevent Viet Minh infiltration of arms and supplies by sea. During the early stages of the war the Viet Minh chartered a number of aircraft and ships to smuggle weapons and supplies either purchased on the open market or supplied by other Asian countries. These ships and aircraft were unmarked. However, French intelligence agents learned of their activities by maintaining surveillance of certain ports and airfields in neighboring Asian countries, including The Philippines. After lodging formal protests with the respective governments, French authorities ordered air and naval forces to fire on any aircraft or ship which violated French territory. After a number of aircraft and vessels were destroyed while trying to run the French blockade, the Viet Minh abandoned this method of obtaining supplies. The nationalities of the crews of the destroyed aircraft and ships remain a mystery and French records give no indication if they were ever identified.

In October of 1949, China fell to Mao Tse-tung and the Viet Minh gained an inviolable sanctuary where they could re-equip, rest, and train their forces without fear of French intervention. In January of 1950, China and the Soviet Union recognized the DRV and began supplying the Viet Minh with increasing amounts of arms and ammunition. Through out the spring and summer of 1950, General Giap trained his troops in the safety of their Chinese base camps in preparation for his first major offensive. That Fall, General Giap launched a major attack against French positions all along Vietnams northern border. Despite air support and paratroop reinforcements, the French were unable to hold. Desperate for help, the French appealed to the United States for military aid.

The low ceiling behind this P-63C was but one of the many hazards faced by French pilots flying in Indochina. Clouds often obscured high peaks and aircraft were lost when they flew into the sides of cloud shrouded mountains. (ECPA/SHAA)

Armorers re-load the nose .50 caliber machine guns of a P-63C of GC I/5. The Kingcobra, despite its age, was well liked by French pilots and its 37MM cannon proved to be a formidable ground support weapon. GC I/5s unit insignia is carried on the car-type door of this Kingcobra and is the same as that carried on Mirage F1C jet fighters that the squadron flys today. (ECPA/SHAA)

The *Criquet* was also used for casualty evacuation because of its ability to land and take off in a short distance. Air evacuation did much to improve a soldiers chances of survival, but the *Criquet* could only be used on airstrips. Helicopters would be better suited for casualty evacuation, but the French had few helicopters available to them. (ECPA/SHAA)

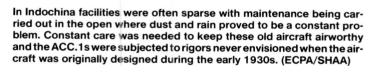

In Indochina facilities were often sparse with maintenance being carried out in the open where dust and rain proved to be a constant problem. Constant care was needed to keep these old aircraft airworthy and the ACC.1s were subjected to rigors never envisioned when the aircraft was originally designed during the early 1930s. (ECPA/SHAA)

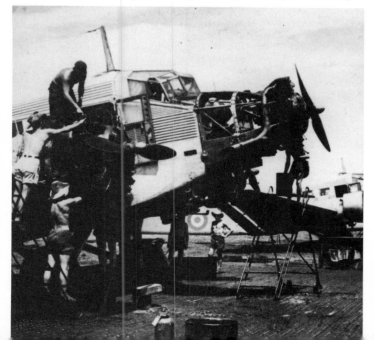

American Aid

U.S. policymakers had been reluctant to support French efforts to restore colonial rule by force and had shied away from providing direct military aid. However, the fall of China and American involvement in the Korean War led to increasing American fears of a communist takeover of all Asia. During the Spring of 1949, France installed Bao Dai (the former Vietnamese Emperor) as head of State of Vietnam. In response to Chinese and Soviet recognition of the DRV, the United States recognized the State of Vietnam as well as the Kingdoms of Laos and Cambodia on 7 February 1950. Nine days later the French officially requested American military aid. President Truman viewed the expansion of communism in Asia as a direct threat to American interests and authorized military aid to the French under the Mutual Defense Assistance Progam (MDAP). The U.S. military assistance program would have three goals; respond to emergency French requests to meet the immediate threat, improve French military capabilities, and develop the indigenous Vietnamese armed forces. In June 1950 the first American aircraft to be supplied under the MDAP, eight Douglas C-47 transports were delivered to Saigon by American crews.

To replace old, worn out fighters, the French immediately requested additional P-63C Kingcobras, primarly because of the P-63s 37MM cannon. However, since Kingcobras were unavailable* forty-eight Grumman F6F-5 Hellcats were provided to re-equip GC II/9 *Auveigne*, GC II/6 *Normandie Neimen*, and GC I/6 *Corse* (formerly GC III/11 which had been redesignated during July of 1947). A number of Hellcats were late model F6F-5s with an alternative armament of two 20MM cannons replacing the two inboard wing .50 caliber machine guns (although the majority of the Hellcats carried the standard armament of six .50 caliber machine guns). With the capability of carrying 2000 pounds of bombs and six 5 inch rockets the Hellcat was ideally suited for the air to ground war.

The Bell P-63 Kingcobra had been out of production since 1945 and although over 3,000 had been produced, only 300 had been delivered to the U.S. Air Force. The Kingcobra had been produced primarily as an export fighter and the majority (over 2,400) had been supplied to the Soviet Union, a highly unlikely source of additional P-63s for the French.

Following the Viet Minh border offensive during late 1950 the French began to receive American military. Grumman F6F-5 Hellcats were the first fighter delivered and were used to re-equip two fighter groups, GC I/6 *Corse* and GC II/9 *Auvergne*. This Hellcat, believed to be from GC I/6, would soon be replaced by another Grumman design, the F8F Bearcat. (ECPA/SHAA)

Because the F6F was no longer in production or first-line U.S. Navy service, there insufficient numbers of Hellcats available to standardized all the fighter units. As a result, the Hellcat was intended to be an interim fighter pending the arrival of a second Grumman design, the F8F Bearcat. The Bearcat was being withdrawn from front-line U.S. Navy squadrons and was selected to be the primary fighter supplied under MDAP. The Bearcat would be modified with a revised fuel system for service with the *Armee de l'Air* and deliveries to Indochina began during February and March of 1951. In the event, over 120 Bearcats would be supplied to the French under the designation F8F-1D equipping GC I/6 *Corse*, GC III/6 *Roussilton*, GC I/9 *Limousin*, GC I/21 *Ariois*, GC II/21 *Auvergne*, GC I/22 *Saintogne*, and GC II/22 *Languidoo* *. After delivery, the French further modified the F8F replacing the radio with an SCR 300 radio for improved air-to-ground communications. A locally fabricated camera pod was developed for use in the reconnaissance role replacing the belly tank on Bearcats assigned to *Escadrille de Reconnaissance Outre-Mer* (Overseas Reconnaissance Squadron) EROM 80.

The Bearcat was well received by *Armee de l'Air* pilots, who appreciated its power, speed, maneuverability, and short take off and landing characteristics. This latter characteristic was especially useful since it enabled the French to operate fighters from the small advance airstrips of *air-heads* (an outpost supplied and supported by air); such as Dong Hoi, La San, and Dien Bien Phu. The Bearcat did have drawbacks; its range with a useful load allowed only a limited loiter time over distant targets, the gyro-compass often failed, the tail wheel would often tear up the pierced steel planking (PSP) at advanced airstrips, and the lack of heavy armor protection made it vulnerable to ground fire. However, the major problem which faced French pilots flying the Bearcat was their own inexperience. Most had been flying the Bell P-63, an aircraft with a tricycle landing gear, and out of habit often made landing approaches in a tail-high attitude. Since the Bearcat was a tail wheel aircraft with a large diameter propeller, this often led to crash landings and a number of Bearcats were damaged during transition training.

*

GC II/21 earlier designated GC II/9
GC I/22 earlier designated GC I/8
GC II/22 earlier designated GC II/8

A line-up of F8F-1D Bearcats of GC I/6 *Corse* based at Bach Mai airfield near Hanoi. The earlier Hellcat was intended as an interim fighter and was soon replaced by the newer Grumman F8F-1D Bearcat which was being phased out of U.S. Navy service. Eventually the F8F would became the main fighter of the *Armee de l'Air* in Indochina. (USAF)

Expansion

The *Armee de l'Air* had long realized the need for light bombers in Indochina, but had none available until the American aid program made the availability of suitable bombers a reality. Under MDAP, the *Armee de l'Air* immediately requested twenty-five Douglas B-26 Invader light bombers. Even though the Invader was in high demand by USAF units in Korea, the United States granted the French request and the first four B-26s arrived at Tan Son Nhut on 4 November 1950. Before the Invader's arrival, the majority of the bombing missions had been flown by fighters, although on numerous occasions both the AAC.1 and C-47 had been pressed into service as makeshift level bombers.

The first unit to be formed with the B-26 was *Groupe de Bombardement* I/19 *Gascogne* stationed at Tourane (later renamed Da Nang). With the B-26 the French were now able to field a relatively modern bomber force which could strike targets far beyond the range of their fighters. The Invader's 6,000 pound bomb load and up to fourteen fixed forward firing .50 caliber machine guns plus gun pods, made the aircraft ideally suited for the ground support role. The French received three variants of the Invader; the B-26B (gun nosed), the B-26C (glass nosed) and the RB-26C (photo reconnaissance). Eventually, 110 B-26s would be supplied under MDAP and equip GB I/25 *Tunisie*, GB I/91 *Bourgogne*, besides the original GB I/19 *Gascogne*. RB-26C reconnaissance aircraft would equip *Escadrille de Reconnaissance* (ER) II/19 *Armagnac* *. Both the six and eight nose gun versions of the B-26B were employed by French squadrons.

Problems with fumes and vibration, led the French to delete the two forward firing nose guns from the glass nosed B-26Cs and these bombers usually were fitted with under wing gun pods to increase forward firepower. With no aerial opposition, the upper turret was traversed forward and controlled by the pilot and the lower turret was deleted, since it proved nearly useless for strafing. The new aircraft was well liked by French crews for its range, speed, firepower, maneuverability, and payload. It gave them an outstanding weapons systems to carry the war to the elusive Viet Minh and often meant the difference between a remote outpost surviving a guerrilla attack or being overrun.

The transport element was also modernized with enough C-47s being supplied under MDAP to allow the French to retire the old AAC.1 from frontline combat duty. The goal of the MDAP to improve French military capabilities was slowly being realized. The supplies of new American aircraft made it easier to standardize maintenance and supply, however, there would continue to be a shortage of maintenance personnel throughout the war. The increased efficiency of the *Armee de l'Air* raised the number of aircraft available for sorties, and expanded sortie rates from an average of 450 a week during the summer of 1950 to 930 a week by the spring of 1951. As the number of Viet Minh casualties inflicted by air attacks grew, the guerrillas became more camouflage conscience and began to upgrade their anti-aircraft defenses.

* Later redesignated Escadrille de Reconnaissance Photographique II/19 (ERP II/19)

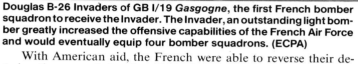
Douglas B-26 Invaders of GB I/19 *Gasgogne*, the first French bomber squadron to receive the Invader. The Invader, an outstanding light bomber greatly increased the offensive capabilities of the French Air Force and would eventually equip four bomber squadrons. (ECPA)

With American aid, the French were able to reverse their deteriorating ground situation. Following his victory along the border General Giap pushed out of the mountains toward Hanoi and Haiphong. In January of 1951, Giap launched a massive attack against Vinh-Yen, followed, in March, by an offensive toward Mao-Khe. Supported by waves of fighters and bombers, the French Army held and soundly defeated Giap's forces, inflicting over 10,000 casualties. C-47s shuttled supplies and troops throughout the fighting and the *Criquet* adjusted artillery fire and performed in the forward air controller role, spotting enemy troop concentrations for air strikes. It was this use of tactical air support that allowed the French to gain a victory, and without it, there is little doubt that Giap would have overrun the French positions and captured the entire area. Giap learned an important lesson and would never again expose his troops to such concentrated firepower.

Buoyed by this victory and revitalized with an increasing flow of American aid, the French regained the initiative and went on the offensive. In operations such as *LOTUS*, *LORRAINNE*, and *CAMARGUE**, paratroops were dropped ahead of mechanized units to seize and hold objectives until relieved. Supported and supplied totally by air, the paratroopers often acted as a blocking force in hopes of trapping sizeable Viet Minh formations. Unfortunately, the dense jungle slowed the mechanized forces and made it difficult to corner the elusive guerrillas. Their familiarity with the countryside usually enabled the Viet Minh to evade French forces and slip away.

* Against Hoa Binh, Phu-Tho and Routel respectively.

The influx of new aircraft, coupled with ground reinforcements, enabled the French to take the offensive against the Viet Minh. One tactic was to establish *air-heads* (outposts supplied and supported by air) deep in enemy territory. It was hoped that these outposts would entice the Viet Minh into the open where superior French firepower could decimate them. One of the most successful *air-heads* was Na San, where the French inflicted a crushing defeat on the Viet Minh. A C-47, believed to be from GT II/64 *Anjou* waits on the runway at Na San while a B-26 makes a low pass over the base. (USAF)

The B-26 gave the French the ability to strike at Viet Minh targets previously outside the range of fighter-bombers. This B-26C Invader, of GB I/19, is enroute to a strike against targets in the mountains of central Indochina during 1954. At ranges closer to base, the Invader's endurance enabled it to loiter for long periods, supporting ground troops with its heavy firepower. (ECPA)

With total command of the air the French also introduced the concept of *Air-heads*. This tatic entailed dropping a sizeable paratroop force deep in enemy territory, then bringing in additional troops, artillery, and supplies by air to expand the perimeter and build an airstrip. Once completed the airstrip would be used by transports to supply the base and evacuate wounded. Bearcats, with their short field performance, could be deployed to the air-head to provide direct air support. Using this tactic, the French hoped to entice the Viet Minh into a set piece battle where superior French firepower could annihilate them. Initially the tatic met with some success. At the Na San air-head, Giap attacked and tried to overrun the French position. Superior French firepower inflicted severe casualties on Viet Minh forces and Giap was forced to abandon the attack and lay siege to the air-head. The French eventually evacuated the post by air to utilize their resources elsewhere.

Their success at Na San made the French commanders overconfident of their ability to establish and support such positions. As long as the French maintained air superiority and the Viet Minh did not possess heavy artillery and anti-aircraft weapons (to bombard the defenses and close the airstrip) it was a viable concept. The Viet Minh, however, recognizing their weakness began to increase both their field artillery and anti-aircraft strength through Chinese aid. Despite reports of this from French Army Intelligence, the High Command failed to take the new threat seriously.

Despite the influx of American transport aircraft there remained an acute shortage of airlift assets. Whenever the French carried out a major paratroop drop, they were forced to requisition civilian aircraft and pilots to augment their own airlift capabilities. The aircraft usually requisitioned was the Douglas DC-3 (C-47), although on occasion the air force also used Douglas DC-6s, Lockheed Constellations, Bristol 170s, and Leo 631s. The long range DC-6s and Constellations were mainly utilized by Air France, to bring reinforcements and vital cargo from Metropolitan France. The Bristol 170, because of its huge clamshell nose doors, was requisitioned to carry bulky items such as artillery and vehicles into forward strips. This use of civilian aircraft was necessary, but it made it extremely difficult for the French to maintain secrecy prior to a major offensive. Even if the Viet Minh were not aware of the objective, they would be alerted that the French were about to launch an attack.

To further supplement their forces, the French contracted the Taiwan based Civil Air Transport (CAT) company, founded by General Claire Chennault, to provide additional transport aircraft and pilots. While on the surface CAT was a legitimate business, it had the covert backing of the U.S. government through the Central Intelligence Agency (CIA). A number of CAT pilots were 'retired' U. S. Air Force officers who flew with CAT as a cover for intelligence gathering missions. Their mission was to two fold, to support the French effort (without directly involving U.S. military personnel) and relay their observations and impressions of the situation in the event a decision had to be made to commit American forces to the area. Flying a variety of aircraft, including Curtiss C-46s, Douglas C-47s and the new Fairchild C-119 Flying Boxcar, CAT crews proved extremely valuable in augmenting the hard pressed French transport crews.

Based on American experience in Korea, the French began using helicopters in the casualty evacuation role. Primarily employing the Westland S-55 (Sikorsky H-19), the helicopter proved invaluable in evacuating casualties from remote outposts to rear areas for medical treatment. Unfortunately, financial limitations prevented the French from deploying the necessary numbers needed and the few H-19s and Hiller H-23s that were available were in constant demand. Occasionally, the H-19s were also used for resupply, rescue, and insertion of commando forces on special missions, but this was the exception rather than the rule. The French soon realized the helicopter's potential in transporting troops over the vast jungles of Indochina. Helicopters could increase the mobility of their ground forces tenfold, freeing them from roads and the danger of ambush by the Viet Minh. Plans were drawn up to form a helicopter borne force, which French officers felt would return tactical mobility and the initiative to them. In the event, these plans would never be implemented in Indochina by the French, but later in Algeria these same plans were used to form helicopter borne units against Algerian guerilla forces. Fifteen years later Americans would use helicopter borne forces against communist forces in South Vietnam with devasting effect*.

* For additional information on U.S. Helicopter forces in Vietnam, see author's 'AIRMOBILE, THE HELICOPTER WAR IN VIETNAM' by Squadron/Signal Publications.

The French received a number of Fairchild C-119 Flying Boxcars on loan from the USAF. The C-119 was well suited for paratroop drops because of its huge rear clamshell doors. In addition to French crews, pilots from Claire Chennault's Civil Air Transport (CAT) Company also flew the Boxcars on a contract basis. The C-119s were assigned to a special detachment which operated from airfields near Hanoi and Tourane (later Da Nang). (ECPA/SHAA)

Dien Bien Phu

By 1953 the war had reached a stalemate with neither side strong enough to force a decision on the battlefield. In an attempt to break the deadlock, the French commander, General Henri Navarre decided to establish an air-head at Dien Bien Phu, deep in enemy territory. Dien Bien Phu controlled the main Viet Minh supply route from Loas and by cutting this route, Navarre hoped to entice General Grap into a set-piece battle. In such an engagement, superior French firepower could be brought to bear to break up the Viet Minh main force. Overconfident because of their previous successes with this tactic the French launched the attack on 20 November 1953. The initial paradrop assault used sixty-four C-47s to lift the 800 man 1st Colonial Paratroop Battalion and its supplies. Initial resistance was light and by the end of the day, Dien Bien Phu was in French hands. Additional forces and supplies were airlifted into the valley after the original airstrip had been repaired. To lift heavy equipment, the U.S. Air Force loaned the French twenty-two C-119 Flying Boxcars. The transports were ferried to Cat Bi airfield, painted in French markings and flown by French and contract aircrews. The C-119s were instrumental in delivering over two dozen artillery pieces, and huge quantities of supplies. Eventually a number of *Criquets* and F8F Bearcats were to operate on a permanent basis from the airfield in the observation and close air support roles.

After a careful study of the French position General Giap decided to give battle. The Viet Minh military commander told Ho Chi Minh that he could put 50,000 troops around Dien Bien Phu. With Chinese supplied and trained artillery and anti-aircraft units he could close the airstrip and pound the French positions until his troops could overcome the fortress. However, these preparations would take months and require the efforts of thousands of Vietnamese. However, with the French overconfidence and the extreme range of their supply line, the Viet Minh commander felt that the final outcome would be a communist victory.

Over the next five months, both sides jockeyed for position in and around the valley. With superhuman effort the guerrillas moved in over 200 guns and mortars around the fortress without the French detecting their presence. The airlift of supplies into Dien Bien Phu was the outpost's lifeline and to meet the needs of the garrison, at least twenty C-119 and fifty C-47 sorties were required daily. By mid-January 1954, the first threat to the airlift was uncovered when radio intercepts revealed the Viet Minh were stockpiling 37MM rapid-fire Soviet-made anti-aircraft artillery (AAA) ammunition in the hills near the fortress. American anti-aircraft warfare experts were consulted and they made a study of reconnaissance photos of the surrounding area, concluding (wrongly) that there were *no 37MM guns in the area.*

On 12 March 1954, the Viet Minh artillery was unleashed on the fortress. On the 14th, Viet Minh gunners closed the principal air-

Buoyed by their success at Na San, the French established an *air-head* at Dien Bien Phu, near the western border with Laos. Bearcats and C-47s were employed to fly air support and re-supply missions from the outpost's airstrip. The mountains in the distance gave the Viet Minh an excellent tactical position to observe every move within the French parameter. (USAF)

An MS 500 over the mountainous terrain surrounding Dien Bien Phu. While the French dug in, the Viet Minh dragged artillery and supplies through the mountains to positions overlooking the French base. The French did not believe the guerrillas possessed heavy artillery and were surprised when shells hit the airstrip. (ECPA/SHAA)

strip, destroying seven F8Fs, two C-47s, one C-119, four *Criquets,* and two H-19 helicopters on the ground. Ground support could now only come from distant bases and the French aircraft carrier *AEROMANCHES*. Dense AAA fire took a severe toll of the fighters, bombers, and transports which tried to support the garrison. In the first week, an F6F Hellcat and an F8F Bearcat were shot down and five other aircraft were damaged. C-47s and smaller aircraft still managed to sneak into the airstrip to evacuate wounded, however, these missions ceased when an air ambulance C-47 was destroyed by artillery fire on 28 March. Slowly, the communists tightened their hold on the valley and took key positions overlooking the fortress. The French, forced to parachute men and supplies into Dien Bien Phu, found that their drop zones were steadily shrinking and their transports were being subjected to the heaviest AAA fire ever encountered over Indochina. The intense AAA fire forced the transports to make their drops from 8,000 to 10,000 feet, dispersing much of the cargo into Viet Minh territory. It is estimated that one half to two thirds of all supplies fell into enemy hands. *Aeronavale* PB4Y-2 Privateer patrol aircraft were pressed into service as high level bombers in an effort to silence the AAA guns, but despite valiant efforts by both air force and navy pilots, the fire continued unabated.

Eventually, as the situation deteriorated the French requested more American aid. On 3 April the French government asked the United States to fly two battalions of French paratroops to Vietnam, and six C-124 Globemaster transports lifted 514 French troops from Paris to Vietnam. On 5 May another lift by five C-124s transported an additional 452 troops to the war zone. In addition to lifting men and supplies the U.S. Air Force provided the French with tons of munitions. Among the weapons supplied was the *Hail* (Lazy Dog) bomb. This was an early form of cluster bomb that had been developed for use in Korea but was to late to see combat. Each cluster unit weighed 500 pounds and carried 11,200 finned bullets. The *Hail* was designed to be dropped from 15,000 feet and burst at 5,000 feet, spreading its missiles over a wide area. On 16 April, 500 cluster units arrived in Haiphong and the first mission was flown by four PB4Y-2 Privateers each carrying twelve bombs. By 2 May over 450 cluster bombs had been dropped on suspected Viet Minh AAA positions. The attacks were judged to be a success because they forced the Viet Minh to disperse their guns and while not silenced, the volume of fire was deminished.

(Above) Bomber support was available from GB I/25 *Tunisie* at Cat Bi Airfield, but the distance between the two bases limited the Invaders time over the target area. To provide extra forward firepower, these B-26Cs are equipped with underwing gun pods, each mounting a pair of .50 caliber machine guns. (ECPA)

On 23 April, the French requested direct American intervention in form of air strikes by Boeing B-29 Superfortress with either conventional or nuclear weapons under the code name *Vulture*. After a great deal of consideration, the bombing request was turned down although additional material aid was provided. Interestingly, while the request was under study, consideration was given to granting a French request for the loan of ten to twenty B-29s to fly the mission themselves. Although this has yet to be confirmed, a number of B-29s at Clark Air Base in The Philippines were reportedly repainted in French markings in case the go-ahead for the transfer was approved. However, General Navarre had informed Paris that he lacked French aircrews to man loaned B-29s and feared their loss if the Chinese intervened with MiG-15 jet fighters.

General Giap launched his final offensive in early May, and within a week his troops overwhelmed the remaining French garrison. During the battle forty-eight aircraft were shot down, sixteen destroyed on the ground, and 167 were damaged. The last French aircraft lost at Dien Bien Phu was a PB4Y-2 Privateer which was shot down on the night of the French surrender. For an air force as small as the *Armee de l'Air* in Indochina, these losses were astronomical. Along with severe personnel losses, the battle of Dien Bien Phu was as much a defeat for the *Armee de l'Air* as it was for the French Army. With the French defeat, the Viet Minh gained a decisive victory on the eve of the Geneva negotiations convened to determine the future of Vietnam*.

For the 8,000 French survivors of Dien Bien Phu, defeat meant a two month 500 mile forced march into captivity. Only 4000 would survive.

(Above) To support the garrison both *Criquets* and Bearcats were based at the Dien Bien Phu airstrip. Pilots of GC I/22 *Saintonge* relax in the sun awaiting orders for their next support mission. The Bearcats appear very worn and scuffy. (ECPA)

(Below) Supplies being loaded onto a C-119 for an airdrop into the besieged fortress at Dien Bien Phu. Unfortunately the Viet Minh already controlled most of the key outer positions greatly restricting the drop zones (DZ). The danger imposed by intense anti-aircraft fire caused many crews to miss the DZ and two-thirds of all airdropped cargo fell into enemy hands. (ECPA/SHAA)

After Dien Bien Phu the Viet Minh were able to concentrate their forces to move on Hanoi and Haiphong. The French Government directed the French commander to withdraw the remaining troops of the Expeditionary Corps south to the 18th parallel, to safeguard the southern portion of Vietnam. As the Viet Minh continued their military victories, discussions in Geneva between representatives of France, the DRV, the United States, the United Kingdom, the State of Vietnam, Russia, Communist China, Laos, and Cambodia dragged on through June and early July. Finally, on 21 July, an agreement was reached. The French agreed to withdraw from all of their former colonies, granting them total independence. Vietnam was divided along the 17th parallel, into the Democratic Republic of Vietnam in the north and the Republic of Vietnam in the south. Elections to re-unify the nation and select a single national government were scheduled for July of 1956, in the event these elections would never take place.

During the remainder of 1954, French units prepared to return home for re-assignment or disbandment. The B-26 Invaders and C-119 Flying Boxcars on loan were returned to the U.S. Air Force and a number of *Criquets* and Bearcats were turned over to the fledgling South Vietnamese Air Force. By 1955, nearly all *Armee de l'Air* units had left Indochina except for GT I/64 *Bearn* which continued to operate from Tan Son Nhut in support of the few remaining French forces left in the area. During July 1956 GT I/64 was finally withdrawn marking the end of *Armee de l'Air* operations in Indochina.

(Above) During the siege of Dien Bien Phu, F8Fs armed with bombs and napalm, flew strikes against the encircling Viet Minh. Although revetments were available, the Bearcats were usually only parked in them at night. When the actual battle began on 12 March the airstrip was quickly closed and most of the Bearcats destroyed on the ground. (ECPA)

(Above) Towards the end of the siege, Bearcats from southern units were transferred to the battle zone to make up for the heavy losses. GC I/21 *Artois*, which was based at Tourane, deployed north to Bach Mai Airfield, were they joined F4U-7 Corsairs of *Flottille* 14F (14th Carrier Fighter Flotilla), which had replaced two other navy squadrons decimated in the fighting. (ECPA/SHAA)

(Below) The French tried to use helicopters based in Laos to evacuate casualties but heavy enemy fire made this nearly impossible, even though the helicopters were marked with Red crosses since the French had used aircraft marked with Red crosses for military purposes and the Viet Minh believed it had a legitimate reason to fire on all aircraft regardless of markings. This Westland S-55 from the 1st Light Medical Evacuation Helicopter Company was lucky. (ECPA)

The Beginning

In Indochina, the French had followed a long standing policy of incorporating native troops into its colonial forces but had resisted creating an independent Vietnamese Military force. During June of 1948, when the French agreed to the formation of both the Democratic Republic of Vietnam (North Vietnam) and the State of Vietnam (South Vietnam) as free states within the French Indochinese Union they decided that a national Vietnamese army in the South would be advantageous. Vietnamese units could augment French units and allow more men to be fielded against the growing Viet Minh. An independent Vietnamese military would also gain support from the United States, where critics were complaining that the Vietnamese themselves were doing little in the struggle against the communist Viet Minh. Additionally, South Vietnamese forces would free French troops to play a greater role in the North Atlantic Treaty Organization (NATO).

The Vietnamese National Army under the leadership of French officers and NCOs grew slowly at first but by 1951 could field some 35,000 regular troops supported by an additional 35,000 auxiliaries. Besides augmenting French Army units, South Vietnamese army personnel were formed into separate Vietnamese units, including an Armored Corps. By 1953, the South Vietnamese Army had grown to over 150,000 men supported by an armored regiment and 50,000 auxiliaries.

The first step toward development of an independent South Vietnamese Air Force (VNAF) took place in June of 1951 when the French opened the Vietnamese Air Training Center at Nha Trang airfield. The Center was staffed by French instructors and equipped with MS 500 *Criquet* observation and liaison aircraft. A month later the Vietnamese Air Force office was officially opened in Saigon and the first Vietnamese squadron, the 1st Air Observation Squadron (1st AOS) was established at Nha Trang. Supposedly an independent unit, the 1st AOS was often used as a source of replacement crews for French squadrons flying the *Criquet*. Although this gave the Vietnamese crews valuable combat experience, it did little to foster moral and underscored the lack of French commitment to an independent Vietnamese Air Force.

During August of 1951, the French transferred a small number of Dassault MD 312 *Flamant* light twin engine transports to the Vietnamese forming a second VNAF squadron, the 312th Special Mission Squadron (312th SMS). Based at Tan Son Nhut the 312th SMS, like the 1st AOS, was formed with crews trained in Metropolitan France and French North Africa. The MD 312s were fitted with underwing bomb racks becoming the first Vietnamese aircraft capable of performing in a limited combat role.

By March of 1952, French instructors had trained a number of Vietnamese pilots, observers and maintenance personnel at the Nha Trang facility, supplementing those trained in France. As Vietnamese aircrews graduated they were assigned to make up for attrition in the two Vietnamese units and to augment personnel in the three French MS 500 squadrons. By early 1953, there were enough

The M.S. 500 equipped the VNAF's 1st Air Observation Squadron based at Tourane (Da Nang). The national insignia consisted of alternating Red and Yellow rings and a South Vietnamese flag marking with alternating Red and Yellow stripes was carried on the rudder. Later VNAF fuselage markings would consist of a variation of the U.S. insignia but the fin flash would remain unchanged, although reduced in size. (USAF)

trained Vietnamese aircrews available to form a second VNAF MS 500 *Criquet* squadron, the 2nd AOS, based at Bien Hoa Airfield. Additionally France, with the concurrence of the United States, began transferring American-made aircraft to the Vietnamese. The MS 500s at Nha Trang were supplemented by the delivery of twenty Cessna L-19 Bird Dog liaison and observation aircraft. The MD 312s were replaced by ten Beech C-45G Expediter light transports, sixteen C-47 Skytrains and a single Republic RC-3 Seabee amphibian with the 312th SMS being reformed as the 1st Liaison Squadron (1st LS). The 1st LS was tasked with shuttling personnel and supplies along the coast between Saigon and the old imperial capitol of Hue, although when the need arose, the aircraft could also be used in the observation role.

During 1953 when the military situation in Indochina had stalemated with neither the French nor the communists being able to achieve a dominant position, the French launched the series of offensives that culminated in their defeat at Dien Bien Phu. When the French realized that their cause was lost they agreed to the future of Indochina being decided in talks at Geneva during the spring and summer of 1954. An agreement was finally reached on 21 July 1954 where French forces would withdraw from all of Indochina with Vietnam being temporarily divided between North and South at the 17th Parallel. Free elections were scheduled to take place in July of 1956 which would reunite the country and elect a single national government.

From the beginning, the Geneva agreement was doomed to failure and two separate and distinct Vietnams began to emerge. In the Democratic Republic of Vietnam (DRV) the communist dominated forces of Ho Chi Minh quickly moved to consolidate their position eliminating all opposition. The brutal collectivization programs conducted by the communist government in the North during 1954 and 1955 led to a mass migration southward of over a million Vietnamese. In the South, the government appointed Ngo Dinh Diem as President of the Council of Ministers. Diem's government received the backing of the United States and announced it would not be bound by the Geneva Accords since free elections could not be held in the communist controlled DRV. With U.S. support President Diem moved to consolidate his government and forestall any attempt by the communists to take over South Vietnam. The various Vietnamese military units which had operated under French control were transferred to Diem's government forming the nucleus of the new South Vietnamese armed forces.

The official transfer of aircraft from French to South Vietnamese control took place on 1 July 1955 and this date is considered to be the official birth of the South Vietnamese Air Force (VNAF) even though the Republic of Vietnam was not proclaimed until 26 October. The aircraft received by the Vietnamese, however, amounted to little more then a token force, numbering only fifty-eight aircraft. These included two squadrons of L-19s, a newly formed C-47 transport squadron, a few M.D. 315s, and an assortment of light liaison and transport aircraft. These aircraft were based at Tourane (later renamed Da Nang), Nha Trang, Bien Hoa, and Tan Son Nhut.

July 1955

Bien Hoa:	1st Liaison Squadron (L-19)*
	Air Force Depot
Nha Trang:	2nd Liason Squadron (L-19)
Tan Son Nhut:	1st Transport Squadron (C-47)

* Moved to Tourane (Da Nang) in November of 1955.

During the early development of the VNAF the French and United States both envisioned that the fledgling Air Force would be an internal security force capable of providing limited liason, observation, and transportation services to the Vietnamese Army (ARVN). Later, an additional transport squadron and a fighter squadron would be added to bolster existing units, but the VNAF was not intended to be a combat force capable of providing extensive and widespread air support across the entire country. In the event such support was needed it was planned that members of the South East Asia Treaty Organization (SEATO) would provide it.

This was a period of transition for the VNAF. The United States provided much of the VNAF's equipment under the Mutual Defense Assistance Program (MDAP) but training was still conducted by the French, assisted by a few Vietnamese instructors. During February of 1955, the United States assumed responsibility for training of all Vietnamese military personnel. French contract officers would, however, continue to fill advisor and training positions within the VNAF until November of 1956, when President Deim decided not to renew their contracts. The Training Center was augmented with the arrival of fifty-five North American T-6G Texan trainers at Nha Trang to begin an advanced training course, and additional training facilities were established to train Vietnamese maintenance, supply and air traffic control personnel. U.S. advisors, operating under the control of the U.S. Military Assistance Advisory Group (MAAG) would slowly become involved with virtually every aspect of VNAF operations.

South Vietnam's refusal to participate in the reunification elections scheduled for July of 1956 led American officials to expect a military reaction from the DRV. In preparation for the expected North Vietnamese invasion, the South Vietnamese military was re-enforced. For the VNAF, these reinforcements included a second transport squadron (2nd Air Transport Squadron) and the first Vietnamese fighter squadron.

An F8F conversion training program had been established earlier at Vung Tau under French contract personnel to train Vietnamese pilots and twenty-five F8Fs relinquished by the French to U.S. control were presented to the VNAF under MDAP. On 1 June 1956, the 1st Fighter Squadron was officially activated at Bien Hoa, becoming the first VNAF combat squadron. Additionally, a Special Mission Unit was formed at Tan Son Nhut consisting of a single L-26 Aero Commander, three C-47s, and three C-45s. The Special Mission Unit was tasked with carrying out overseas flights, liaison and, transportation of government VIPs.

During 1956, the VNAF also established its first rotary-wing unit, the 1st Helicopter Squadron (1st HS) based at Tan Son Nhut. Initially the squadron, although fully staffed, had no helicopters assigned. Vietnamese pilots were assigned to a French H-19 squadron, which was providing transportation services to the International Control Commission (ICC), to gain experience in helicopter operations. Two years later, during April of 1958, the French squadron withdrew from Vietnam and transferred ten H-19s to the Vietnamese.

By the summer of 1958 the VNAF was composed of the following squadrons:

Da Nang:	1st Liaison Squadron (L-19)
Bien Hoa:	1st Fighter Squadron (F8F)
Tan Son Nhut:	1st Transport Group
	1st Transport Squadron (C-47)
	2nd Transport Squadron (C-47)
	Special Mission Squadron (Aero Commander, C-47, C-45)
	1st Helicopter Squadron (H-19)
Nha Trang:	2nd Liason Squadron (L-19)
	T-6 Training Unit

The change of training and advisory responsibility from the French to the Americans resulted in little change in the basic structure of the VNAF. Training now took place at Nha Trang, U.S. bases in The Philippines, or in the United States. American advisors soon discovered that VNAF pilots were good, but young, inexperienced and few appeared to have mastered basic combat skills. Other weaknesses were in command, logistical, and staff functions. These weaknesses were not surprising, considering how the French had dominated the VNAF during its early development and that no Viet-

During the summer of 1951, the French opened a training center at Nha Trang for Vietnamese Air Force personnel. Other Vietnamese pilots were trained in France and French North Africa. Pilots from the first graduating class from the Nha Trang training center pose in front of an M.S. 500 *Criquet*, the French built version of the Fiessler Fi 156 *Storch*. (ECPA/SHAA)

A number of Dassault MD 312 *Flamant* light transports were transferred to the Vietnamese to form the 312th Special Mission Squadron. Armed with underwing bomb racks the *Flamant* was the first combat capable VNAF aircraft. (Dassault via Waters)

namese had been allowed to rise to command rank. American advisors made efforts to help VNAF personnel overcome these problems while changing the VNAF organization from old French procedures to an American system. However, the majority of the problems could only be eliminated with experience and unfortunately, the time needed to gain this experience was rapidly running out.

(Above) A 1st Fighter Squadron F8F Bearcat on display at Tan Son Nhut during 1967. The Bearcat was the first fighter operated by the VNAF and were *ex-Armee de l'Air* aircraft relinquished by the French during 1956.

(Below) During 1958 the VNAF received a number of H-19 helicopters from the French. The H-19 was used to equip the 1st Helicopter Squadron, but were in such poor condition that they did little to improve VNAF airlift capabilities. (USAF)

To upgrade the VNAF, thirty-one Douglas A-1 Skyraiders were delivered between late 1960 and early 1961, to replace the obsolete F8F Bearcats of the 1st Fighter Squadron at Bien Hoa. A lack of spare parts and poor maintenance hindered operational employment of the Skyraiders. (USAF)

Within a year after the deadline for reunification elections had past, Ho Chi Minh realized that he would be unable to reunify Vietnam through peaceful means and ordered a campaign of terrorist attacks against South Vietnamese government officials and installations. Many of these attacks were carried out by former Viet Minh guerrilla bands which had remained in South Vietnam in direct violation of the Geneva agreement. Isolated terrorist incidents and low level guerrilla activity continued throughout 1957, as Hanoi probed the South Vietnamese defenses and attempted to subvert local political organizations.

During early 1958 Ho Chi Minh made a series of diplomatic overtures toward the Diem government, including a personal letter

The 1st Fighter Squadron applied highly decorative bands to the fuselage of their Skyraiders to identify each flight within the squadron. These included a Red devil and flames on a dark Blue background, Black diamonds on a Yellow background, and White arrows on a Red background. (USAF)

from the DRV Prime Minister, Pham Van Dong, proposing high level discussions on troop reductions, trade, and other steps aimed at reunification. Since during the proceeding year the communists had killed or kidnapped over 400 people in South Vietnam the proposal was rejected by President Diem. During May of 1959 the DRV instituted a full scale insurgency designed to bring down the Diem government and reunify Vietnam by force.

North Vietnamese Army General Vo Bam was instructed to infiltrate additional communists agents into South Vietnam who could create a large guerrilla force that could be aided and directed by North Vietnam. General Bam immediately opened the first sections of what would become known as the Ho Chi Minh Trail across the Demilitarized Zone (DMZ), and planned an expansion of the trail through Laos and Cambodia. Supplied via the Ho Chi Minh trail the guerrilla force, now called the Viet Cong (VC) began escalating its attacks against the South Vietnamese government, building its support on the population's dissatisfaction with the corruption, excesses, and religious policies of Diem's rule.

The Vietnamese armed forces were ill-prepared to effectively meet the challenge of guerrilla warfare. The army was organized and equipped to fight a conventional war, the navy was little more than a coastal patrol force, with few craft capable of moving along the rivers

The 1st Fighter Squadron carried the squadron emblem was carried on the cowling and the flight identification band on the rear fuselage. The Vietnamese national insignia and fin flash (on the rudder) were used until the late 1960s, when they were reduced in size, after VNAF aircraft began receiving the three tone camouflage paint schemes. All numbers and letters were painted in Black. (USAF)

and canals bisecting the country, and the air force had little capability to rapidly transport troops in reaction to guerrilla hit and run tactics. Additionally, the VNAF lacked modern fighter or attack aircraft capable of delivering air strikes when enemy troop concentrations were spotted. There was a shortage of trained maintenance personnel and staff officers familiar with modern tactics. The VNAF would require complete modernization and reorganization before it could improve its combat and support capabilities against the rising tide of the DRV sponsored insurgency.

The first concrete step in this modernization took place in August of 1959, following the mysterious crash of an F8F Bearcat of the 1st Fighter Squadron. President Diem grounded the remainder of the obsolete Bearcats and requested immediate jet aircraft replacements from the United States. Although two Lockheed T-33A Shooting Stars and four RT-33A reconnaissance Shooting Stars were promised, they would never be delivered. Restrictions within the Geneva

Accord prohibited the introduction of jet aircraft into Vietnam by either side, and U.S. State Department officials strongly objected to U.S. violation of these provisions. To replace the Bearcats, American officials decided to furnish Douglas AD-4 and AD-6 Skyraiders from U.S. Navy stocks to re-equip the 1st Fighter Squadron at Bien Hoa. The first six Skyraiders arrived in Vietnam during September of 1960 and were followed by an additional twenty-five by May of 1961. Initially the Skyraiders made little impact on VNAF operations since they were usually grounded due to poor maintenance and a lack of spare parts, these problems would plague the VNAF throughout its entire existence. Although Vietnam had at least five airfields capable of Skyraider operations, President Diem prohibited their use, stating that the Skyraiders could not operate effectively at any field distant from the main maintenance facility at Bien Hoa. Purely political, this prohibition was designed to deny potential coup plotters access to air support. Because of the maintenance problems and political restrictions, transition training progressed slowly.

With the help of American advisors the VNAF quickly formed the 2nd Fighter Squadron, equipped with T-28 trainers modified as fighter bombers with underwing pylons and gun pods. This T-28 has just returned to Nha Trang from a training mission during the spring of 1962. (US Army)

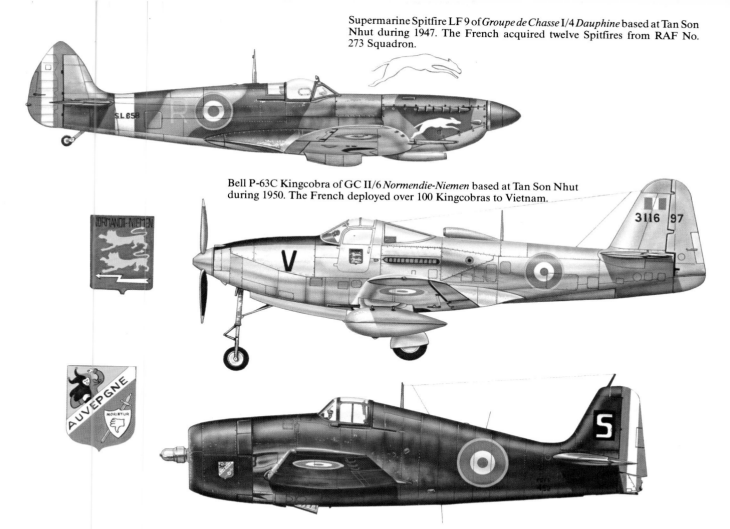

Supermarine Spitfire LF 9 of *Groupe de Chasse* I/4 *Dauphine* based at Tan Son Nhut during 1947. The French acquired twelve Spitfires from RAF No. 273 Squadron.

Bell P-63C Kingcobra of GC II/6 *Normendie-Niemen* based at Tan Son Nhut during 1950. The French deployed over 100 Kingcobras to Vietnam.

Grumman F6F-5 Hellcat of GC II/9 *Auvergne* stationed at Tan Son Nhut during 1952. The Hellcat was used as an interim fighter until replaced by F8F-1D Bearcats.

An *Armee de L'Air* F8F-1D Bearcat in overall Gloss Sea Blue on the ramp at Tan Son Nhut between missions. Each French fighter squadron had a subtle way of identifying their aircraft aside from the squadron crest carried on the nose. The Yellow tail code letter and Yellow edging around the fin flash identify this Bearcat as belonging to *Groupe de Chase* II/21. (Alexander)

This overall green MS 500 *Criquet* carries the Red cross marking of casualty evacuation aircraft. The *Criquet* was well suited for the causality evacuation role because of its ability to operate from small, unprepared landing strips. (Alexander)

1961 - 1962

By late 1961 plans were underway to increase both the size and effectiveness of the VNAF. The U.S. Secretary of Defense had authorized deployment of sixteen USAF Fairchild C-123 Provider transport aircraft to augment VNAF transport squadrons, a second VNAF fighter squadron had been formed, and the number of U.S. advisors had been increased. Steps were also taken to increase radar coverage over South Vietnam, both for air traffic control and to improve the VNAF air defense system. As more aircraft, both American and Vietnamese, began operating in South Vietnamese airspace, traffic control had became a serious problem. Increasing the number of radar facilities improved training for VNAF controllers and the establishment of an Air Operations Center considerably improved the situation.

The improved air defense warning system immediately began picking up unidentified aircraft, particularly along Vietnams northern borders with North Vietnam and Cambodia. Both U.S. and VNAF aircraft were vectored against these radar contacts, but no sightings or engagement ever occurred. Ironically, the first real test of the air defense system came when two VNAF A-1 Skyraiders, piloted by disgruntled officers, carried out a bombing attack against the Presidential Palace on 26 February 1962. The A-1s had been scheduled for a routine mission in the Mekong Delta but broke away from their flight shortly after take off. Two flights of A-1s from the 1st Fighter Squadron were scrambled to intercept the rebels, but both were able to evade interception and bomb Diem's palace. One aircraft was shot down by ground fire and its pilot captured, but the other pilot managed to escape to Cambodia were he crash landed at Phnom Penh. Although there appeared to be no plot to overthrow Diem, the VNAF was immediately grounded. Interrogation of the rebel pilots revealed that they were engaged in a personal vendetta against Presi-

On 26 February 1962, two disgruntled VNAF pilots from the 1st Fighter Squadron bombed the Presidential Palace in Saigon. Though unsuccessful, Diem was so angered by this attack that he ordered the 1st FS Skyraiders grounded. The order was quickly recinded but aircraft operating near the capital were placed under strict guidelines and control. (USAF)

dent Diem's brother and no anti-government plot existed within the VNAF. The grounding order was recinded, but for a long period A-1s in the vicinity of the capitol could only carry 20MM cannon ammunition.

On the battlefield ground fighting intensified, increasing calls for VNAF air strikes. To increase its reaction and loiter times the 2nd Fighter Squadron at Nha Trang deployed a detachment of T-28s to Da Nang. From Da Nang the T-28s could provide the much needed air support for the northern and central regions of Vietnam. The worsening ground situation, however, meant more requests for air support than the VNAF could handle. Even with the assistance of the *Farm Gate* detachment the situation remained critical. Plans were quickly implemented to both increase the size of the *Farm Gate* detachment and send more Vietnamese pilots to the U.S. for flight training. Consideration was even given to assigning thirty Nationalist Chinese pilots to the VNAF. The Nationalist pilots would free up Vietnamese C-47 pilots for combat training. The plan, however, was politically unacceptable and never got beyond the initial stage.

One of the major problems of VNAF ground support was lack of adequate communication and coordination between air and ground units. Because there were insufficient numbers of pilots and observers to man the L-19 observation aircraft available, the VNAF could not provide Forward Air Controllers (FAC) to ARVN ground units on anything like a regular basis. U.S. advisors reported that VNAF observation crews were the least proficient flight crews in the VNAF since the best pilots were assigned to either fighter or transport squadrons. VNAF FACs also operated under severe constraints which hindered their effectiveness; if a FAC aircraft should be

During the spring of 1962, the 2nd Fighter Squadron was declared operational and began to fly combat missions from Nha Trang Air Base. This group of T-28s are on ground alert at Nha Trang awaiting orders for the next air strike against the VC. (USAF)

The 2nd FS adopted a Tigers head as its squadron insignia, which was usually painted on the fin. This T-28 piloted by Capt Pham Long Suu, the squadron commander, is returning from a mission near Nha Trang during 1962. The national insignia on the wing has faded. (USAF)

A pair of VNAF T-28s over a rugged portion of the Vietnamese coast south of Nha Trang during a training flight. These aircraft lack the Tigers Head insignia on the tail and from their relatively clean appearance are probably recently delivered aircraft. (USAF)

damaged by ground fire, the FAC pilot could receive a severe reprimand; if an observer erred in marking a target resulting in friendly casualties, he could be punished or even jailed. It was not surprising that many VNAF FACs flew at high altitudes and consistently dropped smoke markers wide of the target in order to protect themselves. In spite of these handicaps the presence of a L-19 FAC over a convoy or train often deterred the VC from attacking it. The VC and NVA had a healthy respect for airpower.

Unfortunately, this respect for airpower led the Viet Cong to substantially increase the anti-aircraft capabilities of their cadre units during late 1962. As the VC introduced heavier AAA weapons the toll of U.S. and VNAF aircraft lost or damaged by ground fire began to climb. Helicopter gunships were introduced by the U.S. Army in an attempt to provide suppression fire for helicopter-borne forces, but gradually the permissive environment which had existed in the air changed as the VC continued to increased their firepower. Tactics were continually revised to lessen the impact of new VC AAA weapons, but losses continued.

The VNAF was faced with an inability to accurately pinpoint communist targets for air strikes and in an attempt to upgrade VNAF reconnaissance capabilities, U.S. advisors repeatedly requested that the VNAF be provided with Lockheed RT-33A reconnaissance jet aircraft. This was blocked by State Department officials who continued to site the Geneva Accords against the introduction of jet aircraft into the region. As an alternative, eighteen RT-28s, three RC-47s, and two RC-45s were to be delivered and used to form the 716th Composite Reconnaissance Squadron at Tan Son Nhut. The first two aircraft delivered were RC-45s and, while waiting for the remain-

der of their aircraft the 716th's pilots flew strike missions with standard T-28s. During December of 1963 the squadron was officially activated and by mid-1964 was fully operational. During the 716th's transition training, U.S. Air Force RF-101 Voodoos and Army OV-1 Mohawks carried out the reconnaissance mission over South Vietnam.

During late 1962 the VNAF was evaluated by both the USAF and the Royal Australian Air Force (RAAF). Both reported that, although the VNAF had made important strides in modernization and increasing aircraft availability, the VNAF was far from reaching its full potential. The Vietnamese were flying about a third of the missions possible, and during bad weather, weekends, and night, flying fell off drastically. On many occasions the Vietnamese were content to let *Farm Gate* aircraft fly combat missions while VNAF aircraft remained safely on the ground. Leadership had been greatly weakened by the rapid expansion of the air force. But the lack of initiative on the part of VNAF pilots was a far greater problem and was much bigger than expected even under these conditions of rapid expansion. But the VNAF had shown recent progress, increasing sortie rates and improving the quality of aircraft maintenance. Additional steps were of course needed to improve the overall effectiveness of the VNAF but as 1962 ended the VNAF's overall situation appeared to steadily improving.

Inadequate air-ground coordination resulted from a lack of well trained Forward Air Controllers (FACs). Usually poorer pilots were assigned to FAC squadrons and operated under the possibility of punishment of mistakes which further hampered their effectiveness. These L-19s of the 1st Liaison Squadron are based at Bien Hoa. (USAF)

To improve VNAF reconnaissance capabilities, a reconnaissance squadron equipped with RC-45s, RC-47s, and RT-28s was formed. A new RT-28 of the 716th Composite Reconnaissance Squadron is parked on the ramp at Tan Son Nhut shortly after delivery during late 1963. The RT-28 was unarmed and carried a camera pod mounted under the fuselage. (USAF)

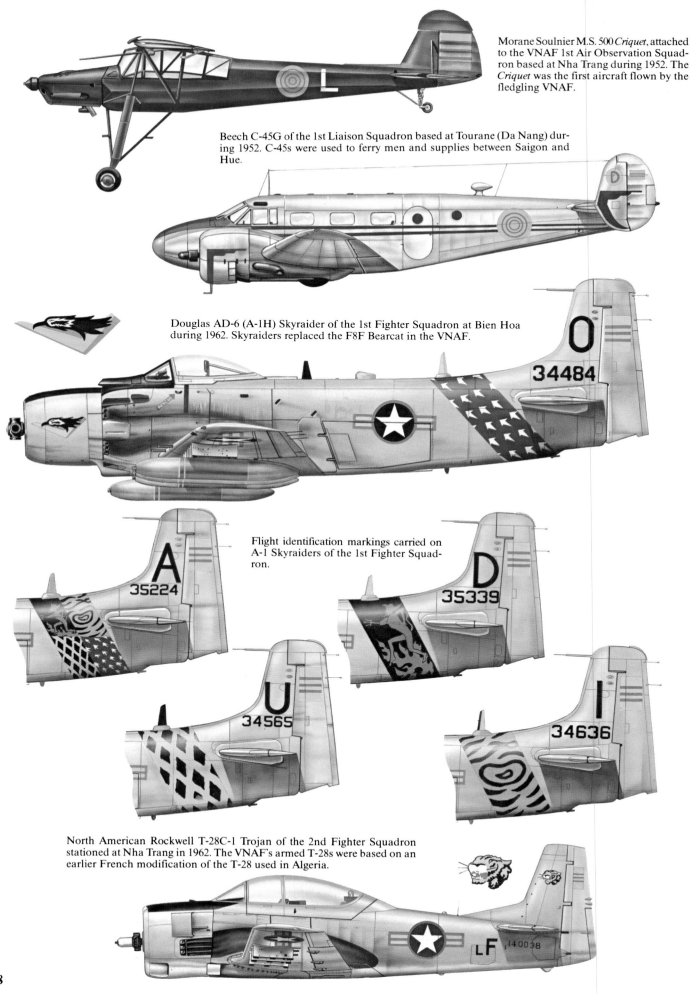

Morane Soulnier M.S. 500 *Criquet*, attached to the VNAF 1st Air Observation Squadron based at Nha Trang during 1952. The *Criquet* was the first aircraft flown by the fledgling VNAF.

Beech C-45G of the 1st Liaison Squadron based at Tourane (Da Nang) during 1952. C-45s were used to ferry men and supplies between Saigon and Hue.

Douglas AD-6 (A-1H) Skyraider of the 1st Fighter Squadron at Bien Hoa during 1962. Skyraiders replaced the F8F Bearcat in the VNAF.

Flight identification markings carried on A-1 Skyraiders of the 1st Fighter Squadron.

North American Rockwell T-28C-1 Trojan of the 2nd Fighter Squadron stationed at Nha Trang in 1962. The VNAF's armed T-28s were based on an earlier French modification of the T-28 used in Algeria.

Sikorsky H-19 Chickasaw of the 1st Helicopter Squadron, Tan Son Nhut Air Base during 1963. H-19s were the first helicopters operated by the VNAF.

527594

North American Rockwell T-28C Trojan of the 1st Air Commando Squadron located at Tan Son Nhut during early 1963. The 1st Air Commando Squadron arrived in Vietnam as part of the *Farm Gate* program.

My Louise

38361

TL361

Douglas EA-1E Skyraider converted to A-1E configuration by the 514th Fighter Squadron, 23rd Tactical Wing at Bien Hoa during 1967. VNAF aircrews disliked the A-1E because of the reduced visibility from the multiplace cockpit.

WB

132487

Three VNAF T-28 Trojans of the 2nd Fighter Squadron armed with bombs and rocket pods on ground alert. VNAF T-28s can be identified by the South Vietnamese fin flash carried on the rudder. *Farm Gate* T-28s carried either a Blue lightning bolt insignia on the fin, or were unmarked. (Chenoweth)

B-26 Invaders of the *Farm Gate* detachment at Ton Son Nhut following the disastrous South Vietnamese defeat at Ap Bac during 1963. *Farm Gate* flew both the six and eight nose gun versions of the B-26B. (Chenoweth)

Changes

During early 1963 the VNAF renumbered its existing squadrons, supposedly to 'confuse' the Viet Cong. The single digit unit identification system was replaced with a three digit system, with the first number identifying the type of unit.

1	Liaison units	2	Helicopter units
3	Special Mission units	4	Transport units
5	Fighter and Attack units	7	Reconnaissance units
8	Combat/Gunship units	9	Training units

Under this system, existing VNAF squadrons were re-designated as follows:

Old	New	Base
1st Fighter Squadron	514th Fighter Squadron	Bien Hoa
2nd Fighter Squadron	516th Fighter Squadron	Nha Trang
1st Liaison Squadron	110th Liaison Squadron	Da Nang
2nd Liaison Squadron	112th Liaison Squadron	Tan Son Nhut
3rd Liaison Squadron	114th Liaison Squadron	Da Nang
1st Transportation Sqn	413th Transportation Sqn	Tan Son Nhut
2nd Transportation Sqn	415th Transportation Sqn	Tan Son Nhut
1st Helicopter Squadron	211th Helicopter Squadron	Tan Son Nhut
2nd Helicopter Squadron	213th Helicopter Squadron	Da Nang

1963 began with a devastating defeat for the South Vietnamese Armed Forces at the village of Ap Bac. In late December of 1962, intelligence indicated that a VC unit was located at the village of Ap Bac and ARVN decided to launch a major armor/airmobile attack hoping to trap the VC and score an easy victory. Unfortunately, the strength of the VC force had been underestimated, what was thought to be a company turned out to be a battalion. When ARVN began the airmobile assault on 2 January, the VC raked the landing zone with heavy automatic weapons fire. Unable to suppress the volume of VC fire, the ARVN commander finally called in VNAF air support. Repeated VNAF air strikes failed to silence the heavy fire and it was not until a *Farm Gate* B-26 made repeated bombing and strafing runs against the enemy positions that the VC broke off contact and slipped away. The final tally revealed just how badly ARVN had been defeated, only a few guerrillas were killed but the VC had shot down five helicopters, damaged a number of aircraft, and killed nearly seventy ARVN troops and U.S. advisors. This was the first time a VC unit had stood and engaged a large ARVN force backed by armor and air support, marking a significant change in VC tactics.

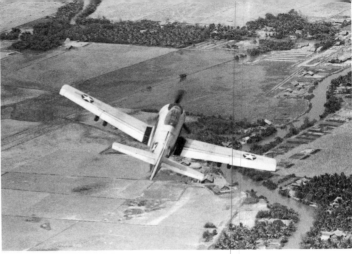

At the village of Ap Bac ARVN engaged a VC battalion dug in and armed with automatic weapons. The VC stood up to the superior ARVN force backed by armor, artillery, and air support. The VC escaped after inflicting heavy losses on the South Vietnamese and their American advisors. This VNAF T-28 rolls in for a firing pass in an attempt to suppress the heavy VC ground fire. (US Army)

The VC were well dug in at Ap Bac and VNAF bombing and strafing runs failed to dislodge them. When a *Farm Gate* B-26 arrived on target and began its attack the enemy disengaged and slipped away. The battle of Ap Bac highlighted many of the command and control problems which plagued ARVN. (USAF)

(Below) Three VNAF H-19s practice formation flying as part of their advanced training. Many of the these pilots later went on to become instructors in the expanding VNAF helicopter program. (USAF via Bell)

(Above) Although the T-28 performed well as long as the VC lacked heavy anti-aircraft weapons, losses to VC AAA fire led to a decision during the spring of 1964 to replace the T-28 with A-1 Skyraiders. These T-28s of the 516th FS are returning from a mission over the rugged Central Highlands region. (USAF)

Because of a fear of punishment for bringing back a damaged aircraft, Vietnamese pilots were often unwilling go low enough to ensure accurate bombing. This T-28, armed with gun and rocket pods takes off from Soc Trang on a ground support mission for ARVN troops in the Mekong Delta. (US Army)

(Above) In January of 1963 a sixty-man USAF advisory detachment arrived at Tan Son Nhut to train VNAF helicopter pilots on the H-19. This US instructor gives the 'OK' signal to a trainee as he lifts an H-19 from the helo pad at Tan Son Nhut. ALthough still marked with *U.S. Air Force*, this H-19 already carries Vietnamese national insignia. (USAF via Bell)

(Below) Gradually the VNAF began to increase its helicopter strength replacing the older H-19s with H-34s that were able to carry more troops. These H-34s are from the 1st Helicopter Squadron at Tan Son Nhut during 1964. (USAF)

The VNAF operated at least three Sud Avaition Alouette III helicopters to support the International Control Commission (ICC) during the early and mid 1960's. The Beech C-45 behind the overall Dark Green Alouette III is a VIP transport. (Chenoweth)

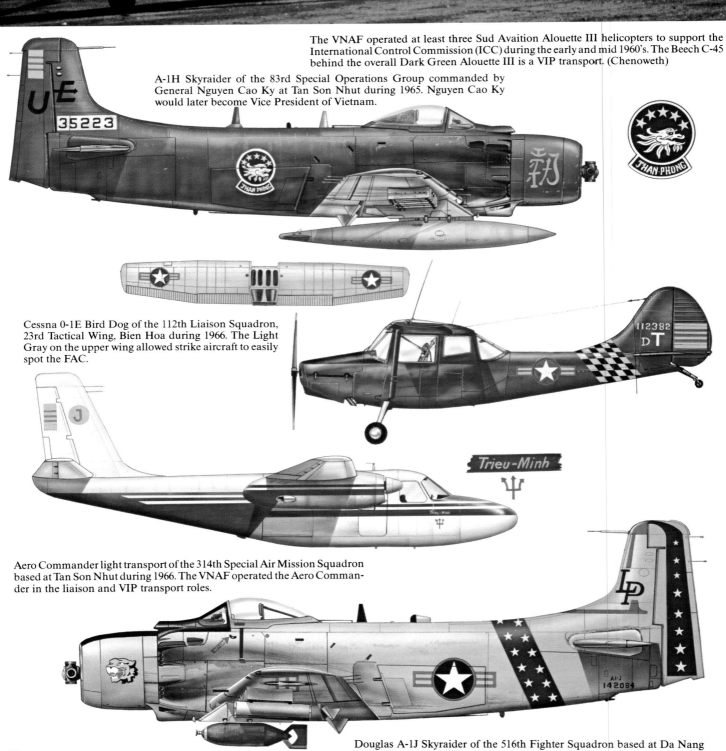

A-1H Skyraider of the 83rd Special Operations Group commanded by General Nguyen Cao Ky at Tan Son Nhut during 1965. Nguyen Cao Ky would later become Vice President of Vietnam.

Cessna 0-1E Bird Dog of the 112th Liaison Squadron, 23rd Tactical Wing, Bien Hoa during 1966. The Light Gray on the upper wing allowed strike aircraft to easily spot the FAC.

Aero Commander light transport of the 314th Special Air Mission Squadron based at Tan Son Nhut during 1966. The VNAF operated the Aero Commander in the liaison and VIP transport roles.

Douglas A-1J Skyraider of the 516th Fighter Squadron based at Da Nang during October of 1966 carrying the 41st Tactical Wing identification band.

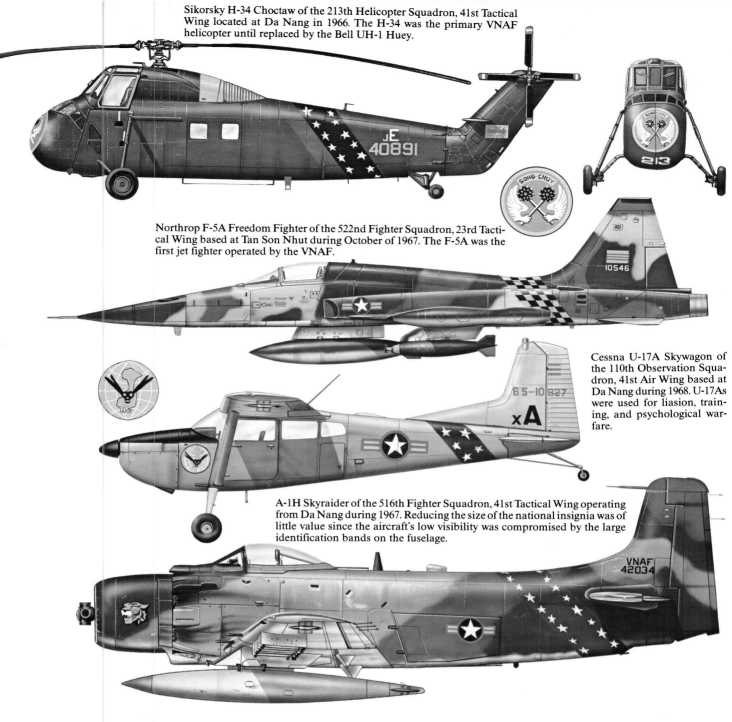

Sikorsky H-34 Choctaw of the 213th Helicopter Squadron, 41st Tactical Wing located at Da Nang in 1966. The H-34 was the primary VNAF helicopter until replaced by the Bell UH-1 Huey.

Northrop F-5A Freedom Fighter of the 522nd Fighter Squadron, 23rd Tactical Wing based at Tan Son Nhut during October of 1967. The F-5A was the first jet fighter operated by the VNAF.

Cessna U-17A Skywagon of the 110th Observation Squadron, 41st Air Wing based at Da Nang during 1968. U-17As were used for liasion, training, and psychological warfare.

A-1H Skyraider of the 516th Fighter Squadron, 41st Tactical Wing operating from Da Nang during 1967. Reducing the size of the national insignia was of little value since the aircraft's low visibility was compromised by the large identification bands on the fuselage.

A C-47 transport of the 314th Special Mission Squadron based at Tan Son Nhut. The 314th SMS had some of the cleanest, best maintained aircraft in the entire VNAF and transported high ranking government officials throughout Vietnam. (JEM Aviation)

This VNAF U-6 Beaver carries an unusual pattern to the camouflage just forward of the national insignia — a very shapely female figure has been silhouetted. Artwork was seldom found on VNAF aircraft but it is doubtful that the lady was an accident. (JEM Avaition)

(Above) In addition to replacing the T-28s of the 2nd FS, new fighter squadrons were also formed with Skyraiders. Vietnamese personnel work on A-1Es and A-1Hs of the newly formed 520th FS at Bien Hoa Air Base. The unit's insignia, a Black panther, is carried on the cowling of the multi-seat A-1E. (USAF via Bell)

(Above) As the VNAF made internal changes squadron markings would be phased out in favor of Wing recognition bands that identified aircraft of a particular Wing and base, rather than an individual squadron.

(Below) The same A-1 now carries the Yellow and Black checkered fuselage band of the 23rd Tactical Wing based at Bien Hoa. The practice of Wing markings was adopted as the number of VNAF squadrons increased making it impractical to allow each squadron to develop its own different recognition markings on their aricraft. (USAF)

At Ap Bac, the performance of each element of the South Vietnamese force left much to be desired and the VNAF had to assume its share of responsibility for the defeat.

Following Ap Bac, additional U.S. aid and advisors were dispatched to shore up the faltering South Vietnamese armed forces. USAF C-123 transports were assigned to augment the Vietnamese C-47s while RF-101s and RB-26s supplemented existing reconnaissance assets. During late January, a sixty man USAF detachment arrived at Tan Son Nhut to train VNAF personnel on the H-19 helicopter. During late summer a similar unit established an 0-1E Bird Dog training center at Nha Trang. Plans were also in place to increase the number of fighter squadrons and replace the T-28 with Douglas A-1 Skyraiders.

Unfortunately, despite this influx of aid and advisors, the VNAF still did not operate to its full ability. There were instances where aircraft remained on the ground when they were critically needed for casualty evacuation or air strikes, forcing U.S. airmen to risk their lives doing jobs that the VNAF should have been doing. At other times VNAF pilots performed heroically but this seemed to be the exception rather than the rule. Support for outlying hamlets improved as C-47 flare ships were used to provided illumination during VC night attacks but many times VNAF fighters failed to come to the aid of a besieged hamlet. During the day, VNAF FAC aircraft often escorted convoys or trains and scared away would-be ambushers, but the 0-1s were too few to provide the escorts needed across the entire country.

On the ground the Viet Cong began to increase the tempo of the war and the number of VC attacks increased. As their operations expanded the VC became more vulnerable to air attacks. To counter South Vietnamese air superiority the guerrillas added heavier anti-aircraft weapons and soon began to take a heavy toll of both U.S. and VNAF aircraft and helicopters. The VC increased ground and mortar attacks on airfields in order to destroy as many aircraft on the ground as possible, both for military and propaganda purposes. This upsurge in guerrilla activity came at a time when the South

(Below) The buildup of VNAF assets included new aircraft such as this Cessna U-17A Skywagon seen on a training flight near Nha Trang. The U-17 would eventually be used in a variety of roles by the VNAF; including liasion, observation, psychological warfare, and VIP transportation. (USAF via Bell)

Vietnamese were actually decreasing their overall effort against the communists. ARVN tended to rely more on air power to carry the war to the enemy, but the VNAF was less willing to shoulder a greater share of the fighting, despite U.S. aid and advisors.

In part, this lethargically attitude could be traced to the ineffective and corrupt leadership of President Diem. During the spring and summer of 1963 dissatisfaction with Diem's government grew and further hampered the war effort. As U.S. support for Diem began to waver, a group of general officers decided that Diem had to be removed from power if South Vietnam was to survive. On 1 November 1963 the plotters, backed by army and air force units, launched a coup against Diem. Four VNAF A-1s and two T-28s made repeated air attacks against the presidential compound which finally fell to Vietnamese marine and airborne forces, although Diem managed to escape. The next day he surrendered, but was murdered while being returned to rebel headquarters.

The coup resulted in a significant change for the VNAF. A new commander, Colonel Nguyen Cao Ky, was appointed head of the VNAF as a reward for the support he had provided during the coup. A brave and charismatic pilot, with a taste for brightly colored flight suits and scarves, Ky was probably one of the most dynamic young officers in Vietnam. A natural leader, he quickly raised moral in the VNAF by personally leading air strikes against the VC. Within American circles he soon earned a reputation as a 'fighter', although his outspoken statements, especially in later years, caused a certain amount of furor within political circles. He immediately began pressing for a buildup of the VNAF and especially wanted jet aircraft. A firm believer in centralized control, Ky fought various attempts to have individual squadrons assigned directly to Corps commanders, since they often misused the aircraft at their disposal.

Following Diem's ousting, the new government attempted to halt the deteriorating war situation with a new offensive posture. Air attacks on suspected guerrilla targets increased, especially in the Cambodian border regions. During one of these missions, a USAF 0-1E Bird Dog was shot down by Cambodian T-28s after it allegedly crossed the border. Both the U.S. pilot and Vietnamese observer were killed. During early 1964 the VNAF again reorganized. As the number of squadrons had grown, it had become necessary to organ-

(Above) Additional fighter units made it possible to provide each corps area with a squadron to insure adequate and timely support. These Skyraiders from the 516th FS sit on a rain soaked ramp at Da Nang during the 1964 rainy season. When the 516th converted from T-28s, the Tiger's head insignia was moved to the cowling of the A-1. (USAF)

The Blue band with White stars of the 23 Tactical Wing is carried on this H-34 of the 213th Helicopter Squadron at Da Nang. Although attempts were made to standardize Wing markings, squadrons did not always rigidly adhere to painting instructions.

ized them into wings, with each wing being assigned to a particular base.

Bien Hoa	23rd Tactical Wing	Can Tho	74th Tactical Wing
Da Nang	41st Tactical Wing	Pleiku	62nd Tactical Wing
Tan Son Nhut	33rd Tactical Wing		

US advisors reported that VNAF H-34 crews refused to fly missions into areas of known heavy ground fire. These reports were suppressed by both the US and South Vietnamese governments. These H-34s are from the 211th Helicopter Squadron, believed to be the unit involved. (USAF)

A trio of A-1H Skyraiders armed with bombs and napalm enroute to a target in the Mekong Delta. The Skyraiders appear to have been recently painted in the South East Asia camouflage scheme of Dark Green, Medium Green, and Tan over Light Gray despite the heavy exhaust staining on the fuselage sides.

Cessna A-37B Dragonfly of the 524th Fighter Squadron, 62nd Tactical Wing, 2nd Air Division located at Nha Trang during 1969. The A-37B gradually replaced the A-1 as the VNAF's main fighter-bomber.

Cessna U-17A Skywagon of the 114th Liaison Squadron, 62nd Tactical Wing, 2nd Air Division based at Nha Trang during August of 1969.

A-37B of the 520th Fighter Squadron, 74th Tactical Wing, 4th Air Division at Binh Thuy during 1970. A-37s were well liked by VNAF aircrews for their agility and load carrying capability.

A New War

After the *Gulf of Tonkin Resolution*, direct American participation in the war became a reality. As additional American aircraft arrived in-country, VNAF airfield facilities quickly became grossly over-crowded. With American aid and manpower, air bases were expanded and facilities upgraded to handle the influx of new U.S. units. With the expanded American presence came additional men and material which indirectly assisted the VNAF with its supply and maintenance problems. Earlier requests for expansion of the VNAF were acted upon and the VNAF soon underwent a rapid growth in organizational units, types of aircraft, and flexibility. Replacements of lost A-1s kept fighter squadrons up to full strength, and additional C-47s improved airlift capability and the number of 0-1Es per unit was increased to provide enough aircraft for a FAC to be assigned to each division. New aircraft, such as the Cessna U-17A Skywagon and deHavilland Canada U-6 Beaver were provided and used for liaison, psychological warfare, VIP transportation, and movement of supplies to and from forward airstrips.

During early 1965, the VC still held the initiative in the ground war and the South Vietnamese political situation remained in turmoil. A succession of governments, some civilian and some military, each tried to provide effective leadership, however, the end result was near chaos. As the situation continued to deteriorate, American combat troops were introduced during March of 1965, initially to provide security for sensitive installations. Gradually the American presence grew and eventually began to move out into the field on combat missions.

During this period of political turmoil, General Ky had used the VNAF to thwart attempts by various factions to impose governments which were not to his liking. Eventually, his dissatisfaction with the political situation led Ky to join with other young officers to bring

This A-1H of the 518th FS is painted in the new three tone camouflage scheme of Dark Green, Medium Green and Tan over Light Gray. Eventually the large national insignia would be reduced in size to make the aircraft less conspicuous in the air. (USAF)

Fighters were not the only aircraft to carry camouflage. Although some VIP transports such as this C-47 of II Corps Commander General Vinh Loch carried colorful paint schemes, most C-47s were quickly repainted in the new South East Asia camouflage colors.

This C-47 of the 415th TS, has been recently repainted in the three tone camouflage scheme designed specifically for American tactical aircraft in Southeast Asia. (USAF via Bell)

A number of A-1s carried a more subdued camouflage scheme without national insignia. These A-1s were used by the VNAF for clandestine missions over Laos and Cambodia. It is believed that most, if not all of these Skyraiders were assigned to the 83rd Special Group. (Menard)

The VNAF received new aircraft for liasion, VIP transport, and psychological warfare. This U-17A Skymaster from the 110th Liasion Squadron was based at Da Nang and carried the Blue band with White stars of the 41st Tactical Wing. (Hansen via Mutza)

down the civilian government which had taken over from General Khanh in February of 1965. Ky was appointed Prime minister in June and was able to bring stability to the chaotic political conditions which had so far prevailed. A special unit of hand-picked politically reliable pilots loyal to Ky manned an elite flight of A-1s stationed at Tan Son Nhut to provide support against any possible coup attempt. Although this diversion of aircraft insured Ky's survival, it lessened the number of aircraft available for use against the VC whenever tensions ran high in the capital and there were rumors of a possible coup.

With General Ky in control of the government the VNAF, for obvious reasons, began receiving substantially more support. Ky continually pushed for additional aid to enhance the VNAF, which dovetailed with American planning for an increased American commitment to the war.

Yet in a way, the increased U.S. involvement in the war, although bring material help, caused the VNAF to become somewhat complacent. With the arrival of large numbers of Army, Air Force, and Marine Corps air units, the actual burden of fighting the war shifted to the Americans. The VNAF continued to fly missions, but the majority of combat now fell on U.S. units which were better equipped, and better motivated. Additionally, whenever possible both ARVN and U.S. ground units requested American air support in preference to VNAF air support, since it was usually quicker to respond and more accurate in delivery. The willingness of U.S. units to fly as much as needed, coupled with the VNAF's acceptance of the situation, did not bode well for the future, and helped lay the groundwork for many of the problems which later surfaced.

To counter the increase in VNAF strength and activity, the Viet Cong began carrying out mortar and rocket attacks against air bases. This H-34 was damaged by a mortar round at Binh Thuy, a major base southeast of Saigon in the Mekong Delta. (US Army)

An A-1 of the 520th FS takes off with a full load of bombs for a strike against a VC target in the Mekong Delta. General Ky's leadership, both militarily and politically did much to raise moral and bring stability to the government.

that the C-121 would be unsuitable as a gunship because of its poor maneuverability, difficult crew egress, vulnerability to ground fire, and the high cost of modification and operation. C-121 maintenance requirements were also felt to be beyond VNAF maintenance capabilities. The SYSCOM study concluded that the AC-119G would be the best aircraft available to expand the VNAF gunship fleet.

During early 1971, the USAF 17th Special Operations Squadron (SOS), the sole USAF unit equipped with AC-119Gs, was ordered to begin a training program for VNAF air crews. The three phase training program consisted of ground school, instrument flying, and combat tactics. Vietnamese crews selected for AC-119G conversion first attended a C-119 flight orientation course at Clinton County AFB in Ohio. When qualified on the C-119 VNAF crews then converted to the AC-119 at Phan Rang. During April of 1971 the first eighteen member VNAF *Shadow* class graduated at ceremonies attended by Vice President Nguyen Cao Ky.

The VNAF AC-119 program made rapid progress as additional AC-119Gs and maintenance equipment were turned over to the Vietnamese. On 24 September, the last AC-119 was officially presented to the VNAF and the 17th SOS was officially relieved by the VNAF's 819th Combat Squadron. The new VNAF AC-119 unit immediately began flying combat missions from Tan Son Nhut freeing USAF gunship squadrons for operations over the Ho Chi Minh trail.

(Above) Following the success of the VNAF AC-47 program, steps were taken to equip a second VNAF gunship squadron with the AC-119G Shadow. Training for VNAF crews was undertaken by the 17th Special Operation Squadron based at Phan Rang. These Vietnamese students are practicing on the AC-119's Forward Looking Infrared (FLIR) sensor. Their shoulder patches are those of the 5th Air Division based at Tan Son Nhut which became home for the new VNAF gunship squadron. (USAF via Dana Bell)

(Below) The VNAF's AC-119G gunship squadron became operational on 1 September 1971 at Tan Son Nhut and was designated the 819th Combat Squadron. This AC-119G was one of the first turned over to the VNAF by the U.S. Later under the *Enhance Plus* program the VNAF would receive the more potent AC-119K. (USAF)

47

Vietnamization

To increase VNAF airlift capabilities, the C-119 Flying Boxcar was added to the VNAF inventory during 1968. One C-47 squadron began conversion the C-119 during the summer of 1968 and by November was combat ready. A number of VNAF C-119s were delivered to Bien Hoa still in the USAF color scheme of White over Gray. (Mutza)

During 1966 the VNAF had an inventory of approximately 400 aircraft organized into sixteen squadrons with a total manpower of 15,000 men. Two years later the VNAF inventory numbered approximately 360 aircraft assigned to seventeen squadrons and personnel strength had risen to 16,000. During this period the VNAF had added newer more capable aircraft, such as the F-5 Freedom Fighter, and steadily improved its organization and training to consolidate the growth it had experienced throughout the early and mid 1960s.

The war, although going well for American and South Vietnamese troops on the battlefield, was causing increasing political turmoil in the United States. On 30 January 1968, the reportedly beaten VC launched their Tet offensive, a massive surprise assault on U.S. and South Vietnamese installations across the length of Vietnam. The Tet offensive ended in a crushing defeat for the VC and NVA, virtually destroying the VC as a military force. In the future NVA regulars would be met in the field with increasing regularity. However, Tet led to increased anti-war protests in the U.S., ultimately leading to President Johnson's decision not to seek re-election in 1968. Richard Nixon won the election on a political platform of shifting more of the war's burden to the South Vietnamese. This election platform was put into policy under the Nixon administration's *Vietnamization* program, which would replace American combat units with Vietnamese forces.

For the VNAF, 1968 marked the beginning of a period of unprecedented growth as the United States moved to implement President Nixon's *Vietnamization* program and reduce American involvement in the war. During the summer and fall of 1968 the 413th Transportation Squadron was re-equipped with C-119 Flying Boxcars greatly, enhancing VNAF airlift capability. Selected Vietnamese air crews were sent to the U.S. for training, with others entering a conversion course taught by a special USAF detachment stationed at Tan Son Nhut. By November training had been completed and the 413th TS began flying supply missions with their new aircraft. The C-119 proved to be an excellent aircraft for VNAF needs. It had a larger payload capacity than the C-47, and with its clamshell rear cargo doors, it was easier to load, superior for air-dropping cargo, and was able to handle larger bulkier loads. The C-119's only serious drawback was its poor short and rough field landing characteristics. Flying Boxcars were unable to fly from many of Vietnam's more primitive airfields, especially those used to resupply the Special Force's camps along Vietnam's borders and in the Central Highlands. Nevertheless, the C-119 allowed the VNAF to more than double its monthly cargo lift capacity.

The C-119G Flying Boxcar provided increased payload, ease of loading, and was able to handle bulky cargo through its clamshell rear door. Unfortunately, it did not have good short field performance which limited its ability to resupply outlying border areas and Special Forces camps. (Hansen via Mutza)

Following the success of the C-119 program it was decided to further increase VNAF airlift capability by adding three squadrons of C-123 Providers. Training was carried out both in the U.S. and Vietnam. As crews became qualified they flew missions alongside USAF C-123s. This C-123 of the 421st TS can be identified by the White Q on its tail. A White R was used as an identification letter by the 423rd TS, and a White X identified the 425th TS. All three squadrons were based at Tan Son Nhut. (USAF)

Following the successful C-119 conversion program, plans were formulated to further modernize VNAFs transport squadrons and increase their capacity. These plans called for formation of three Fairchild C-123 Provider squadrons and two squadrons of de Havilland Canada C-7 Caribou transports during 1971 and 1972. Later, a third C-7 Caribou squadron would be added and the number of aircraft in each squadron increased from twelve to sixteen. When this program was completed officials in both Saigon and Washington felt the VNAF would possess enough airlift capacity to fulfill foreseeable demands over the immediate future.

Pilot training for the VNAF C-123 project began during 1970 when forty-eight C-47 pilots were transferred to Lockbourne AFB, Ohio.* C-123 co-pilots were sent to Lockbourne directly from undergraduate pilot training. By early 1971 the first VNAF C-123 crews had finished their training and were assigned to the American 315th Troop Carrier Wing (315th TCW) in Vietnam for additional training and to gain combat experience. VNAF Maintenance personnel were also assigned to the 315th TCW for on-the-job training with both Vietnamese and American instructors. The program progressed smoothly and during April of 1971 the first Vietnamese C-123 squadron, the 421st Transport Squadron (421st TS), was formed. During July, a second squadron, the 423rd TS became operational and by September both units had a combined strength of forty-eight C-123s. Formation of the last squadron, the 425th TS, was completed in December. Personnel for the 425th had received their training directly from Vietnamese instructors, allowing USAF advisors to be reassigned to other programs.

The VNAF C-7 Caribou program followed much the same pattern as the earlier C-123 program. During the summer of 1971 forty-eight pilots drawn from VNAF transport units were sent to Dyess AFB, Texas for C-7 conversion training. Again co-pilots entered the program directly from undergraduate pilot training. Upon completion of their initial training these crews returned to Vietnam and were assigned to the 483rd Troop Carrier Wing at Phan Rang for advanced tactical training. VNAF C-7 maintenance personnel were trained at the Phan Rang facilities used by USAF advisors to train VNAF C-123 students. During January of 1972, the Phan Rang training center was closed and its personnel moved to Phu Cat where C-7 training continued for VNAF groundcrews until August.

Upon completion of advanced training, Vietnamese aircrews were assigned to USAF C-7 squadrons at Cam Ranh Bay for

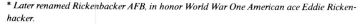

* Later renamed Rickenbacker AFB, in honor World War One American ace Eddie Rickenbacker.

A C-123 of the 423rd TS being refueled at Bien Hoa during December of 1971. Although an excellent aircraft for flying from small forward airstrips, the Vietnamese hesitated to use the C-123s at outlying bases for fear of loosing them to VC ground attacks. (Mutza)

The H-34 was the only troop carrying helicopter in the VNAF inventory but there were never enough for effective use. An H-34 lifts off from the rain soaked runway at Tan Son Nhut for a mission over the Mekong Delta. Many of the VNAF H-34s suffered mechanical problems due to age and poor maintenance, which further reduced their effectiveness. (USAF)

A number of H-34s were used for clandestine missions into Cambodia and Laos under the codename *Kingbee*. This unmarked Black and Olive Green camouflaged H-34, is believed to be from the 219th HS based at Da Nang. (USAF)

Eventually the H-34 was replaced by the Bell UH-1 Huey, the standard American helicopter used throughout Vietnam. This newly delivered Huey is parked on the ramp at Bien Hoa during the spring of 1970 and carries U.S. Army camouflage of overall Olive Drab. Eventually five VNAF UH-1 squadrons would operate from Bien Hoa. (USAF)

To provide the VNAF helicopter force with a medium lift capability the Vietnamese received a number of CH-47 Chinook helicopters during 1970 to form the 241st HS. During 1972, a second Chinook squadron was formed to replace departing American Chinooks. (Chenoweth)

operational experience. The first VNAF C-7 squadron, the 427th TS, was formed at Phu Cat during March of 1972 and over the next four months was joined by two additional VNAF Caribou squadrons, the 429th and 413th Transportation Squadrons. To ease transition a number of USAF pilots and mechanics were assigned to these units until the Vietnamese were able to assume all training and maintenance responsibilities themselves.

During 1968 there were five Vietnamese helicopter squadrons equipped with aging H-34 Choctaw helicopters badly in need of replacement. In preparation for re-equipping VNAF helicopter squadrons with the Bell UH-1 Huey a number of VNAF helicopter pilots were assigned to U.S. Army UH-1 Huey companies both to gain experience with the UH-1 and to study U.S. airmobile tactics. To gain further experience in airmobile assault operations, two VNAF H-34 squadrons were assigned to Binh Thuy Air Base to provide helicopters for large scale ARVN airmobile assaults against VC positions in the Delta.

The results of these training programs were encouraging and during 1969 a number of Vietnamese pilots were trained on the UH-1 at U.S. Army schools in the United States. After graduation these pilots were assigned to various U.S. Army units in Vietnam to gain combat experience before being assigned to a VNAF squadron. The five VNAF H-34 squadrons began converting to the UH-1 Huey during 1970 and later that same year four additional UH-1 squadrons were formed. The VNAF helicopter force continued to be enlarged and ten additional squadrons were formed between 1971 and 1972. Each VNAF UH-1 squadron was equipped with thirty-one helicopters, but unlike the U.S. Army, there were no special gunship units. Instead, each VNAF squadron had a section of eight Huey gunships assigned for escort and fire support during airmobile assaults.

In order to provide the VNAF helicopter force with heavy lift capability, U.S. officials decided to equip the VNAF with one squadron of CH-47 Chinook helicopters during late 1969. The Chinooks would be used for cargo movement, artillery lifts, and retrieving downed aircraft. After a familiarization course in the U.S., Vietnamese pilots were assigned to U.S. Army CH-47 companies to complete their training. The first VNAF Chinook unit, the 241st Helicopter Squadron (241st HS), was activated during 1970 and quickly proved invaluable for supporting ARVN units in the field. The 241st HS was joined during early 1972 by a second VNAF Chinook squadron, the 243rd HS.

By early 1972, the *Vietnamization* program had greatly expanded and modernized the VNAF. The table below shows the gains made in personnel, squadrons, and aircraft when compared to 1968.

(Approximate)	1968	1972	% of increase
Personnel	16,000	47,000	300%
Squadrons	17	47	270%
Aircraft	360	1,300	400%

Vietnamization had provided the VNAF with men, new aircraft, and better training allowing the VNAF to shoulder a greater burden of the war and release U.S. troops for redeployment home or to other assignments. The future looked bright and the policy of *Vietnamization* appeared to be an unqualified success.

Coming of Age

Following the 1968 Tet Offensive VNAF F-5s, A-1s, and A-37s assumed a larger share of the responsibility for air strikes in support of ARVN units. Because of a lack of sophisticated electronic warning and countermeasures equipment, VNAF fighters were unable to mount air strikes against the heavily defended Ho Chi Minh trail. VNAF fighters were, however, employed to strike targets in southern Laos and Cambodia.

During the *Cambodian Incursion* in the spring of 1970 VNAF fighters, helicopters, and cargo aircraft were used to support both U.S. and ARVN troops. This incursion had been specifically targeted against the North Vietnamese Army (NVA) staging areas along the Cambodian border in the 'Parrot's Beak' and 'Fishhook' regions.* These important NVA sanctuaries contained troop concentrations, massive supply dumps, and base camps needed to support NVA operations in the southern portion of South Vietnam.

On 29 April 1970 ARVN attacked NVA sanctuaries opposite the 'Parrot's Beak' and two days later a joint ARVN/U.S. task force attacked NVA positions in the 'Fishhook'. After American ground forces withdrew from Cambodia on 30 June, the VNAF continued to support Vietnamese troops remaining in Cambodia, with little assistance from American units. While little contact with enemy troops was made, the Cambodian operation was a still huge success, enough individual weapons to supply at least seventy-four NVA battalions had been captured along with massive amounts of rice, ammunition, and explosives. During the remainder of 1970, ARVN launched a number of spoiling attacks against enemy positions in Cambodia both to keep the NVA off balance and to aid the hardpressed Cambodian army. The majority of these operations received only minimal U.S. assistance because the Nixon administration, under heavy criticism from a hostile Congress, and the American peace movement, tried to limit American participation in all Cambodian operations.

One of the more ambitious operations carried out by the VNAF was *OPERATION EAGLE JUMP*, an airborne operation to shore up Cambodian forces under heavy NVA and Khmer Rouge attack near Kompong Cham. Although the USAF advisory team had offered to plan the operation, the Vietnamese politely refused the offer and instead formulated their own plans. There was considerable American concern whether or not the VNAF was capable of laying out such an operation, but during the pre-mission briefing American reservations rapidly disappeared as the VNAF plan unfolded.

OPERATION EAGLE JUMP began on 14 December 1970, when VNAF helicopters airlifted an ARVN assault group to secure the airfield at Kompong Cham. Once the airfield had been secured, VNAF C-47s and C-119s began landing additional troops. The landings had to be halted at dusk because Kompong Cham had no runway

The newly activated 522nd FS saw a great deal of action following the Tet Offensive as both US and South Vietnamese forces fought to eliminate communist forces which had finally come out in the open. These three F-5As are armed with a mixed load of napalm and bombs, with external fuel tanks on the centerline and wing tip stations. (USAF)

lights but supply flights continued at first light the next day with a second ARVN battalion and artillery being flown in. Re-supply flights continued on a regular basis until Vietnamese troops were withdrawn in late December. During the two week period of *EAGLE JUMP* the VNAF had not lost a single aircraft, although several were damaged by groundfire. The VNAF had flown 451 sorties into Kompong Cham lifting over 1700 troops and 900 tons of cargo. This achievement was impressive, even more so considering the VNAF accomplished it with negligible U.S. support.

The next major ground operation involving direct VNAF support was *LAM SON 719*, a major assault by ARVN troops into Laos during early 1971. ARVN deployed their best troops in the assault including the Airmobile Division, Marine Brigade, 1st Infantry Division, and the 1st Armored Brigade. On 8 February 1971, 5000 ARVN troops crossed the Laotian border opposite Khe Sanh to seek out and destroy NVA supply dumps on the Ho Chi Minh Trail. The bulk of the helicopter support for this attack, however, was provided by U.S. Army UH-1 Hueys and AH-1G HueyCobras. During the course of *LAM SON 719* the U.S. Army lost 118 helicopters shot down and VNAF lost seven. *LAM SON 719* was a qualified success, and NVA losses were estimated to be over 100 tanks, 405 trucks, seventy-six artillery pieces, and 13,000 troops. ARVN had shown it could stand up to numerically superior forces and with proper support hold its own. During the course of the operation, the VNAF had faced heavy NVA anti-aircraft defenses including radar controlled guns, SA-2 *Guideline* surface-to-air missiles and a new threat, the SA-7 *Strella* man-portable surface-to-air-missile.

The old Skyraider still played an important role in the VNAF. This A-1 of the 23rd Tactical Wing at Bien Hoa has just returned from a mission against enemy positions in War Zone 'D', north of Bien Hoa. The reduced national insignia meant to lower the A-1s visibility, is compromised by the Yellow and Black checkerboard fuselage band of the 23rd Tactical Wing. (USAF)

---

* The 'Parrot's Beak' is a peninsula of Cambodian land which juts into Vietnam thirty-three miles from Saigon and the 'Fishhook' is a curved area of Cambodian territory that projects into Vietnam fifty miles northwest of Saigon.

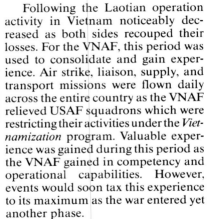

A number of two-seat A-1Es were used by the VNAF but was not well liked by VNAF crews because of reduced visibility from the multi-place cockpit. The expansion of the VNAF raised the numbers of aircraft in service forcing the VNAF to adopt a three letter tail code identification system. (USAF)

Following the Laotian operation activity in Vietnam noticeably decreased as both sides recouped their losses. For the VNAF, this period was used to consolidate and gain experience. Air strike, liaison, supply, and transport missions were flown daily across the entire country as the VNAF relieved USAF squadrons which were restricting their activities under the *Vietnamization* program. Valuable experience was gained during this period as the VNAF gained in competency and operational capabilities. However, events would soon tax this experience to its maximum as the war entered yet another phase.

For approximately a year after *LAM SON 719* Vietnam remained relatively quiet. This quiet was shattered on 30 March 1972 when the NVA launched a series of massive ground attacks across the DMZ, through the Central High-lands, and north of Saigon in what would become known as the *Easter Invasion*. For the first time NVA employed tanks in massed formations which were met by stiff resistance by some ARVN units but the weather denied ARVN close air support. The weight of the NVA assault slowly wore down the defenders and they were forced to withdraw and regroup.

The weather finally improved and VNAF tactical aircraft, assisted by U.S. squadrons rushed to the combat zone, flew hundreds of sorties against the advancing NVA. The NVA had incorporated large numbers of anti-aircraft missiles and radar controlled guns into their invasion forces which proved a serious threat to both American and Vietnamese aircraft. In combat areas where the NVA used sophisticated anti-aircraft weapons the VNAF was faced with a severe handicap since VNAF fighters were equipped to fight in a more permissive air environment and lacked electronic countermeasures equipment. In these areas more advanced U.S. aircraft flew the brunt of support missions, while the VNAF concentrated on less hostile areas. Nevertheless, the VNAF lost a number of A-1s, A-37s, C-123s and C-119s to shoulder-launched SA-7 missiles during the defense of Quang Tri.

At An Loc and Kontum, VNAF UH-1s suffered a particularly high casualty rate. Sixty-three Hueys were lost and another 391 suffered major damage; accounting for over 70 percent of the VNAF helicopter force. This was the highest attrition rate ever suffered by the VNAF. Although VNAF performance had been impressive, some ARVN commanders complained that helicopter crews lacked initiative and a few had demonstrated outright cowardice. This complaint is not borne out by the high helicopter losses, yet under the circumstances, there is probably some truth to the claim. On the whole, the performance of VNAF crews was outstanding and they achieved remarkable results under very difficult conditions.

Gradually the A-37 replaced the A-1 in a number of squadrons or were used as initial equipment for new squadrons. This A-37 of the 524th FS carries a mixed load of 500 and 750 pound bombs during a mission over the Central Highlands. The intake screen designed to keep foreign objects out of the engine intake is retracted under the fuselage during flight. (USAF)

U-17 Skywagons were used by the Vietnamese in a number of roles including psychological warfare with powerful speakers mounted behind the pilot. This U-17A is believed to be from the 716th RS based at Tan Son Nhut. (USAF)

The U-17A was also used for pilot training at Nha Trang. This student pilot carries out engine checks under the watchful eyes of his instructor and ground crew. (USAF)

The *Easter Invasion* resulted in a recommendation from U.S. Air Force advisors to MACV that VNAF C-47, C-119 and C-123 squadrons be re-equipped with C-130s. MACV endorsed and forwarded this request through channels to Washington where it was immediately opposed by the Secretary of Defense and Joint Chiefs of Staff. Their opposition was based on the time needed to retrain VNAF aircrews on the C-130, a perception that C-130 maintenance requirements were beyond VNAF capabilities, and USAFs own requirements for C-130s. While this request was being discussed, a directive was issued from the White House via the State Department that the VNAF would be provided C-130s!

The White House directive had resulted from talks between South Vietnamese President Thieu and Secretary of State Henry Kissinger. These discussions had centered on what was required to gain Thieu's support for a cease-fire agreement between the warring parties. It was clear to both Vietnamese and American officials that the Vietnamese Armed Forces would require significant amounts of material and equipment to be able to withstand another NVA offensive. Programs were quickly put in motion to build up the South Vietnamese military under the code names Enhance and Enhance Plus. For the VNAF these programs would mean not only a tremendous influx of aircraft and material, but also tremendous problems which would severely tax the Vietnamese Air Force as it prepared to 'go it alone'.

The VNAF participated in a number of operations in Cambodia during 1970 and 1971. Transport squadrons used both C-47s and C-119s to move men and material into the battle zone, allowing ARVN units to stage raids against enemy targets without US aid. This pair of C-47s of the 415th TS are parked on the pierced steel planking at Tan Son Nhut between missions. The camouflage paint quickly faded under the harsh climate and tropical conditions in Vietnam. (USAF)

The weakest arm of the VNAF were the Forward Air Controller (FAC) squadrons. Pilots assigned to FAC duty were under qualified and usually lacked the authority to direct air strikes. These factors contributed to the poor performance of VNAF FACs in combat. This 0-1E from the 116th LS based at Binh Thuy in the Mekong Delta has a White upper wing surface to aid strike aircraft in spotting the FAC. (USAF)

A number of Beavers were employed for psychological warfare. This U-6 is engaged in a mission over the Mekong Delta, the most populated portion of South Vietnam, and an area where the government made a special effort to win the support of the people. (USAF)

A number of U-6A Beavers were supplied to the VNAF for support and liaison roles. The Beaver's rugged construction made it ideal for operating from small, unprepared airstrips at border camps or fire support bases. This U-6 carries the insignia of the 33rd Tactical Wing based at Tan Son Nhut on its cowling. (USAF)

A few U-17As used in the FAC role were fitted with underwing racks for smoke rockets, although this was not a widespread practice. This U-17 carries the markings of the 4th Air Division at Binh Thuy. An old Beech C-45 is parked in the hanger behind the U-17. (USAF)

A smoke rocket armed 0-1E from the 122nd LS taxies from a revetment at Cao Lanh in the Mekong Delta for another FAC mission. The stripes on the rudder are unusual markings for a VNAF aircraft and appear to be Red and White. (US Army)

(Above) A number of UH-1s in each helicopter squadron were modified for the gunship role with rocket pods and 7.62MM mini guns. This UH-1 crew scans the terrain below for any signs of VC activity during a mission near the Cambodian border. The pilot and cargo doors were often removed to save weight and allow for rapid escape in the event of crash landing. (USAF)

(Below) A group of ARVN soldiers load a Huey with supplies for delivery to troops in the field. This UH-1 of the 215th HS whose insignia, a White elephant, is carried on the nose. Although VNAF helicopter units began to shoulder a larger burden of the war during the early 1970s, they did not play a major role in *Lam Son 719*, the Laotian Incursion in early 1971. (USAF)

Enhance and Enhance Plus

While U.S. and North Vietnamese negotiators in Paris continued to work toward a cease-fire, steps were taken to accelerate the upgrading and modernization of the South Vietnamese Armed Forces. Much of this modernization had already been planned but under the terms of the proposed cease fire agreement, deliveries of equipment and material would be severely restricted once the cease fire went into effect. To complete the modernization before the deadline, U.S. officials authorized a massive air and sealift of equipment and material under two programs. The first of these, Project Enhance, was designed to replace material lost during the NVA Easter Invasion, allowing South Vietnam's Armed Forces to meet any future NVA assault. The VNAF's portion of Project Enhance was five F-5As, two squadrons of A-37s, twelve RC-47s, a squadron of AC-119Ks, a squadron of C-7s, a squadron of C-119Gs, two squadrons of C-47s, twenty-eight A-1s, and thirty-two UH-1 helicopters. These new aircraft allowed the VNAF to replace losses, improve tactical support, airlift capability, and upgrade gunship support.

Following on the heels of Project Enhance, which also armed the ground forces, came Project Enhance Plus, which was designed solely to augment and modernize the VNAF. Under this program, the VNAF was additionally provided three squadrons of A-37s, two squadrons of F-5As, two squadrons of C-130s, an AC-119K squadron, three squadrons of CH-47s, three squadrons of UH-1s, ten EC-47s, twenty-four T-37s and thirty-five 0-2s. Enhance Plus also provided for replacement of three squadrons of F-5As with the new Northrop F-5E Tiger II and an increase in the strength of UH-1 units. Furthermore, enough C-130s were promised to eventually replace all C-47s, C-119s, and C-123s in VNAF transport units, and the Cessna 0-2 Super Skymaster was scheduled to replace the O-1E in FAC squadrons.

Over the course of Enhance and Enhance Plus the VNAF received a total of over 700 aircraft and helicopters including: 118 F5A and F-5Bs, ninety A-37Bs, 286 UH-1s, twenty-three CH-47s, twenty-two AC-119s, twenty-eight A-1s, thirty-two C-130s, twenty-three EC-47s, twenty-four T-37s, and thirty-five 0-2s. In order to meet the required number of F-5s needed by the VNAF the U.S. government leased a number of F-5As from Nationalist China, Korea, and Iran. These leased F-5As were to be replaced in VNAF squadrons with F-5E Tiger IIs on a one for one basis as F-5E production increased. The leased F-5As would then be returned to their respective governments.

These re-enforcements brought VNAF strength to over 2000 aircraft, making it one of the world's largest air forces. The VNAF now had sixty-five squadrons and a total strength of 61,147 men. Although these numbers sound impressive, there were inherent weaknesses in the VNAF structure. The most immediate problem was that the VNAF had twenty-five different types of aircraft in their inventory,

To provide sufficient numbers of F-5As, the U.S. leased aircraft from Korea, Iran, and Nationalist China. This F-5 just offloaded from a C-5A transport is camouflaged in the desert scheme used by the Imperial Iranian Air Force. (USAF)

These F-5A fighters, still bearing USAF markings, wait in revetments at Bien Hoa Air Base, northeast of Saigon for repainting and assignment to VNAF fighter squadrons. (USAF)

As quickly as the aircraft were unloaded they were stacked in revetments at Bien Hoa until they could be reassembled and painted in standard VNAF camouflage and insignia. (USAF)

The VNAF received a number of RF-5A reconnaissance aircraft for use in high-risk areas where the EC-47 and RC-47s could not survive. However, the NVA deployment of sophisticated Russian anti-aircraft missiles and radar controlled anti-aircraft guns in South Vietnam severely restricted operation of the RF-5 because it lacked effective electronic countermeasures equipment. (USAF)

Besides F-5s, the VNAF received ninety A-37 light bombers to supplement the 150 already in service. U.S. and Vietnamese personnel guide an A-37 fuselage into a revetment at Phan Rang, home base of the 548th Fighter Squadron, a VNAF A-37 unit. (USAF)

In order to supplement the airlift capability of the VNAF thirty-two C-130As were requisitioned from Air National Guard and Air Force Reserve squadrons. At Tan Son a C-123K taxis past eight C-130s which were part of the initial deliveries. Older transports returned to American control were reconditioned and either returned to the U.S. or supplied to other Asian allies. (USAF)

making maintenance a nightmare for the few fully trained maintenance personnel, and played havoc with the supply system. Planners in both Washington and Saigon felt that the problem could be partially solved by hiring contract maintenance personnel, and eventually standardizing on fewer aircraft types. Standardization would take place as older aircraft were retired and slowly replaced by newer types.

Maintenance problems were compounded by VNAF failure to perform preventative maintenance. VNAF maintenance crews seemed to follow the motto 'if it isn't broke don't mess with it'. Unfortunately, a complex combat aircraft cannot be treated in such a manner for any length of time before it becomes inoperable. The attitude of VNAF mechanics personnel stemmed from their almost total lack of mechanical background, unlike their American counterparts who grew up around machines. Another factor which contributed to poor maintenance was the tremendous growth in the VNAF which had taken place over such a short period of time. Training had been compressed and there was little depth of experience among maintenance crews. This was further complicated by a lack of adequate supervision from crew and maintenance chiefs. These individuals had been promoted faster then warranted and had been unable to gain the necessary supervisory experience to go along with their new responsibilities. Finally the VNAF, except for aircrews, was viewed as a relatively safe job and many wealthy families used money and political clout to have their sons assigned to the VNAF. The motivation of these recruits was low and often affected others around them. These conditions would contribute to the demise of the South Vietnamese Air Force.

In addition to improving VNAF fixed wing transportation capabilities, efforts were made to increase the air lift capability of the helicopter force. Twenty-three CH-47 Chinook medium lift helicopters were supplied for movement of supplies and equipment which were beyond the load limit of the UH-1 Huey. These Chinooks rest on pallets at Tan Son Nhut air base following delivery by USAF C-5A transports. (USAF)

Cease Fire

On 27 January 1973, the Paris Peace Treaty ending American troop involvement in the Vietnam War went into effect. From the beginning the treaty was doomed to failure.

For the VNAF the period immediately following the Paris Peace treaty allowed little time to absorb the new aircraft delivered during late 1972 and early 1973. To increase maintenance levels, older aircraft were placed in flyable storage at various airfields freeing personnel for more important tasks. Combat readiness of the remaining operational aircraft rose since more aircraft were now available for sorties on any given day.

Fighting continued as the NVA probed South Vietnamese defenses and tested American resolve to support the South. These NVA probes often led to fighting on a heavier scale than before the peace treaty was signed. The VNAF played an important role in these battles since air support gave ARVN a decided advantage over the NVA. To counter South Vietnamese air superiority the NVA, in violation of the truce, moved in large numbers of radar controlled heavy anti-aircraft guns, SA-2 surface-to-air missiles, and SA-7 hand-held heat seeking missiles. The SA-7, a small portable shoulder launched missile, posed a significant threat to low flying aircraft and helicopters. During the first six months of 1973 the NVA fired at least twenty-two SA-7 missiles downing five VNAF aircraft and three helicopters. By the end of the year another twenty VNAF aircraft would be lost to SA-7s.

Introduction of the SA-7 altered the balance of power between

The main VNAF fighter bomber was the A-37, a robust and reliable aircraft. Unfortunately, the NVA introduction of the SA-7 hand-held anti-aircraft missile seriously challenged the VNAF's control of the air. This A-37 of the 520th FS heads for a target in the Mekong Delta, ever watchful for the tell tail smoke trail of a missile launch. (USAF)

Although the cease fire supposedly put an end to fighting in South Vietnam the war continued without let up. The VNAF was called upon to provide air support for ARVN units and blunt a number of NVA thrusts. Several VNAF squadrons continued to operate the reliable Skyraider, such as this one of the 518th FS but eventually a lack of spare parts forced the VNAF to place all remaining A-1s into flyable storage. (USAF)

the NVA and VNAF. The VNAF's only available countermeasures were flares and structural modifications to lower an aircraft's infrared signature. VNAF UH-1 Hueys were quickly modified with new exhaust shrouds that directed engine exhaust upward into the rotor down wash, lessening the SA-7's ability to achieve a lock on. F-5s and A-37s carried flare dispensers providing a limited defense against the SA-7, but costing the fighter a weapons station. The SA-7 had stripped away the permissive environment in the air which had existed prior to the 1972 Easter Invasion.

The VNAF was now faced with completely restructuring tactics and operational procedures. Fighters now had to attack from higher altitudes in order to survive, which lessened accuracy. Movement of troops and supplies by helicopter became more dangerous since helicopters were relatively easy targets for the SA-7. Supply missions to besieged camps became especially dangerous for slow flying transports, which in some cases had to be halted. Supplies were now air-dropped from safer altitudes, but this hindered resupply efforts and often resulted in the loss of badly needed cargos that fell into enemy hands.

Throughout 1973, the VNAF was heavily engaged in air support for ARVN ground forces and in air strikes against NVA staging areas. The small outpost of Tong Le Chon, near An Loc, was able to survive an NVA attack only through air support. Over 400 sorties including air strikes and supply drops were flown in support of the camp's defenders. Helicopter operations were severely restricted by heavy NVA ground fire and five helicopter were shot down. In the Central Highlands, C-130s airlifted the entire ARVN 22nd Division

While fighter squadrons had the most visible role in the air war, transports played a vital role in moving men and supplies to counter NVA thrusts. C-130s, such as this Hercules of the 435th TS were important additions to the transport fleet. (Pham Quang Kheim)

Pilot training was carried out at Phan Rang, where students were trained on T-37s and T-41s. The T-37s were flown by the 920th Training Squadron, while the T-41s were assigned to the 12th TrS. The pilot in front of this T-41 is Pham Quang Kheim, who flew his family out of Vietnam in a C-130 just before Vietnam fell. (Pham Quang Kheim)

RF-5's were used to monitor the NVA buildup when RC-47s and EC-47s were forced to abandoned these missions due to heavy ground fire. The RF-5s also suffered losses to the radar directed guns and missiles used by the NVA and gradually the VNAF lost its ability to provide intelligence on enemy strengths and intentions. (USAF)

to Pleiku to counter movements of the 320th NVA Division. Air strikes by F-5s, A-37s, and A-1s were flown against enemy tank and troops concentrations but were largely ineffective since the threat of SA-7s forced VNAF pilots to bomb from higher altitudes and their bombs usually missed the targets by a wide margin. ARVN intelligence reports indicated that NVA gunners had been complaining that VNAF pilots were flying above the range of their 37MM guns. When flying in support of ARVN troops in combat with NVA forces pilots often took great personal risks to deliver their bombs on target, but when flying against targets such as supply dumps and anti-aircraft positions VNAF pilots felt these objectives were not worth the risks involved.

By early 1974 the VNAF realized it was faced with a war of attrition, a war it could not win. Budgetary restrictions had cut the number of flying hours, reduced fuel for non-combat training, and replacements for combat losses were unavailable. These cut-backs meant that fewer missions could be scheduled for hard pressed ground forces who desperately needed air support. The increasing volume of NVA ground fire made pilots cautious and less willing to take risks unless absolutely necessary. There were simply no replacements or spares available for destroyed or damaged aircraft. This led to a decline in morale and the reputation of the VNAF became tarnished in the eyes of the common soldier who often failed to get air support when he needed it most. At other times the VNAF would perform admirably but this now became the exception rather

than the rule. The VNAF could now only respond to direct threats and was unable to carry out offensive actions to thwart a massive NVA build-up now going on.

Throughout the remainder of 1974 the VNAF attempted to blunt NVA assaults against outlying ARVN positions with mixed results. Tong Le Chon, which had held out for over a year, was finally abandoned to heavy NVA attacks which the meager VNAF air strikes were unable to contain. In the Central Highlands a string of ARVN posts fell one after another. Air support, which might have saved some of these, was hampered by intense ground fire and poor weather. These same conditions prevailed in I Corps, where the NVA took a number of important ARVN posts around Hue, Da Nang, and Quang Tri as they continued to tightened their grip on the northern half of South Vietnam. Restrictions on flying time and ordinance prevented VNAF from halting this steady erosion of ground positions vital to the defense of South Vietnam.

By the end of 1974 the VNAF had lost some 300 aircraft to combat, accident, and retirement. Budgetary cuts planned for 1975 forced the reduction of active squadrons from sixty-six to fifty-six and another 224 aircraft were put into flyable storage. Those aircraft now in flyable storage included all remaining A-1s (61), C-7s (52), 0-2s (31), along with a number of AC-47 and AC-119 gunships (34), and UH-1 helicopters (31). As the South Vietnamese grew weaker their opponent seemed to grow stronger. The NVA poured a steady stream of troops, tanks, artillery, and heavy anti-aircraft weapons into the countryside in blatant violation of the peace treaty. The United States did nothing to counter the North Vietnamese. Watergate had toppled President Nixon, and most Americans now felt that the U.S. had done enough for South Vietnam. Congress had passed the Cooper-Church Amendment restraining Presidential authority to re-commit American forces to Vietnam and further cut military aid to the Vietnamese. There was little hope that the new president, Gerald Ford, would be able to change the mood in Congress and restore aid to its former level. Time was quickly running out for the American backed Thieu government unless dramatic changes occurred. The final battle for South Vietnam was only a breath away.

This VNAF CH-47 carries a sling load of supplies to a forward base northeast of Bien Hoa. Helicopters became prime targets for the SA-7 because they usually flew at low altitudes well within missile range. The SA-7 greatly restricted the use of helicopters and denied the South Vietnamese the capability to rapidly shift men and material to meet NVA attacks. (USAF)

Mounting losses and cuts in US aid seriously restricted the VNAFs ability to function and ARVN units desperate for air support received only a fraction of what was needed. An F-5A of the 23rd Tactical Wing stands ground alert in a revetment at Bien Hoa. (USAF)

DERELICT C-7

DERELICT C-47

DERELICT C-119

FOUR 0-1s
ELEVEN 0-2s
TWENTY-ONE A-1s

27

Following the NVA victory at Ban Me Thuot, President Thieu ordered a withdrawal from the Central Highlands. Unfortunately the withdrawal quickly became a rout with the NVA gaining a tremendous victory. A reconnaissance photo taken by USAF reconnaissance aircraft reveals part of the Pleiku airstrip with abandoned aircraft lined up neatly in revetments. The 0-2 FAC aircraft were received by the VNAF but never used. (USAF)

The End

The lack of U.S. military response to repeated North Vietnamese peace treaty violations encouraged the NVA to accelerate their build-up in South Vietnam. The VNAF tried to monitor NVA activity on the Ho Chi Minh trail losing four RF-5s to heavy ground fire, half of the VNAF's tactical reconnaissance aircraft. These losses severely hindered VNAF intelligence estimates of NVA strength and intentions. The hostile air environment created by the influx of radar controlled anti-aircraft guns and missiles allowed the NVA to seriously challenge South Vietnamese control of the air. To reverse the situation the United States would have to either re-commit American airpower or provide the VNAF with more modern aircraft and systems. The first course of action was impossible in the face of heated opposition to any further American involvement in Vietnam. Budgetary restrictions and a lack of experienced personnel made it impractical to re-equip the VNAF with more sophisticated aircraft and ECM equipment. The VNAF would have to use what it had.

North Vietnam, realizing the time was right to achieve its goal of re-uniting Vietnam under communist rule, launched a series of small ground attacks to further test U.S. reaction. When these attacks failed to draw a military response from Washington, the NVA staged a massive attack on the strategic town of Ban Me Thuot in the Central Highlands. Ban Me Thuot controlled Highways 14 and 21, vital supply lines for the important highland towns of Kontum and Pleiku. The NVA had selected the Central Highlands as the battlefield in an attempt to cut South Vietnam in half.

On the night of 9 March 1975, the NVA struck the city and airfield with artillery, mortars, and rockets. By the next afternoon, over half of Ban Me Thuot was in enemy hands, despite fierce resistance from ARVN defenders. VNAF air strikes destroyed five NVA tanks but during one strike, a bomb accidentally hit ARVN sector headquarters, severely disrupting communications. At the airstrip, the small ARVN garrison came under attack and was forced to defend the control tower, preventing attempts to fly in reinforcements. ARVN reinforcements were diverted to Buon Ho, north of the city, far from the battle. On the airfield, the NVA had destroyed an 0-1, a CH-47, and ten UH-1s, although three damaged Hueys had managed to escape to Pleiku. Fierce fighting continued for three more days but by 14 March the situation was hopeless. During the four day battle the VNAF flew over 200 sorties inflicting heavy losses on the NVA, but to no avail. Fortunately no aircraft were lost in the air, but three A-37s at Pleiku were destroyed by 122MM rockets on 11 March when the NVA rocketed the airfield .

The day Ban Me Thuot fell, President Thieu called an emergency high level meeting at Cam Ranh Bay. During this meeting Thieu made the decision to attempt an orderly withdrawal from the Central Highlands around Kontum and Pleiku in order to conserve forces and regroup for a counter-attack. Unfortunately, the commander of the region, General Phu, misinterpreted this order and directed an immediately evacuation of both cities. The commander of the 6th Air Division at Pleiku was given forty-eight hours to evacuate the airfield and immediately requested UH-1s, CH-47s and C-130s to fly VNAF personnel and their dependants out of Pleiku. On 16 March artillery fire began hitting the city and ARVN troops began a retreat to the coast along Highway 7B. At the airfield sixty-four aircraft were abandoned with little effort to destroy them before evacuating and large quantities of fuel and ordinance were left behind, undamaged and ready for the enemy to use. During the retreat a misdirected VNAF air strike decimated a Ranger battalion and threw the entire column into mass confusion. On 25 March, what remained of the column staggered into Tuy Hoa, but within a few days this city was also under fire by the pursuing NVA.

Further north, in I Corps, the disaster in the highlands had a profound effect on the South Vietnamese troops and civilians around Hue, Quang Tri, and Da Nang. Conflicting orders from Saigon caused confusion, lowered morale, and led to troop movements which defied any logic. As rockets and artillery fire began to hit Da Nang Air Base on 28 March, the 1st Air Division was ordered to evacuate. Approximately 130 aircraft managed to evacuate but over 180 were left behind along with huge stocks of fuel and ordinance. Abandoned were thirty-three A-37s, most of which were captured intact by the NVA. By 30 March one of the largest cities in South Vietnam and its huge air field were under communist control.

Coming so soon after the loss of Kontum and Pleiku, the fall of Da Nang caused widespread panic and desertion within the South Vietnamese armed forces. The North Vietnamese, sensing that victory was theirs, deployed their reserves and immediately began pushing south along the coast toward Saigon. Constant pressure was maintained on retreating ARVN forces to prevent them from regrouping or establishing new defensive positions. The long columns of NVA tanks, trucks, troops, and artillery were wide open to air attack but the VNAF ignored them. The few sorties flown were against well defended NVA positions in direct support of ARVN units. Most of the coastal cities fell without resistance although A-37s from Phu Cat and Phang Rang carried out numerous sorties against armored columns converging on Qui Nhon. As the NVA closed in on the airfield at Phu Cat, VNAF ground personnel manned the perimeter defenses abandoned by ARVN troops while pilots loaded their own bombs and fuel on the A-37s. The NVA was so close that pilots often did not have time to retract the landing gear before dropping their bombs. Despite such efforts, the NVA continued to push south and when Phu Cat was abandoned all remaining flyable aircraft were flown to Bien Hoa or Phan Rang.

By the beginning of April, the situation had become critical. Communist forces rapidly pressed on toward Saigon with the remaining VNAF aircraft being concentrated primarily at Bien Hoa, Tan Son Nhut and a number of bases in the Mekong Delta. On 8 April, a renegade VNAF F-5 pilot bombed the Presidential Palace, then flew northeast landing at a communist held airfield where the pilot was hailed as a hero.

At Xuan Loc, a key position covering the approaches to Saigon, Bien Hoa and Tan Son Nhut, the ARVN 18th Division prepared to meet the NVA in a last ditch defense. Xuan Loc would be the last major battle and the VNAF committed what was left of its aircraft. A-1s were pulled out of storage to make up for losses and C-130s loaded 'daisy cutter' bombs, 55 gallon fuel drums full of napalm, 15,000 pound BLU-82 bombs and flew as level bombers. The first NVA attack on Xuan Loc came on 9 April and the 5000 men of the 18th Division held, repulsing 40,000 NVA regulars. The VNAF flew sortie after sortie in support of the besieged city, but without FAC direction many of the air strikes failed to hit their targets. On 15 April a successful NVA rocket attack destroyed or damaged twenty F-5s and A-37s at Bien Hoa. Fighting continued around Xuan Lock as the 18th Division, supported by over 600 sorties by the VNAF, continued to hold. Finally, on 22 April, the last battle in Vietnam ended as the remnants of the 18th Division fell back toward Saigon. The NVA had finally overwhelmed Xuan Loc's defenders by sheer weight of numbers.

The loss of Xuan Loc made Bien Hoa Air base indefensible, although the VNAF continued to fly from the base until enemy artillery fire forced evacuation to Tan Son Nhut. At dusk on 28 April, three A-37s, captured by the NVA bombed Tan Son Nhut destroying a number of aircraft on the flight line. There are conflicting stories about who was actually flying these aircraft. One source insists they were VNAF pilots who were communists, another says they were VNAF pilots who were forced to fly the mission in return for the

safety of their families, and NVA General Van Tien Dung claimed the A-37s were flown by North Vietnamese Air Force pilots. Whatever the case, the A-37s escaped, despite being pursued by several F-5s. Although the physical damage to Ton Son Nhut was not extensive, the threat of further air strikes eliminated Ton Son Nhut for fixed-wing evacuation flights, further lowering what little morale remained in the capital.

Saigon was now surrounded by thirteen NVA divisions and most Vietnamese realized it was only a matter of time until the entire country was in communist hands. On 29 April President Ford ordered *OPERATION FREQUENT WIND* the helicopter evacuation of Saigon. Vietnamese pilots now began flying themselves and their families out of the country in anything that could get off the ground. Some headed for the American rescue fleet just off the coast, while others flew to Thailand. On 30 April, the last desperate combat sorties flown by the VNAF were carried out in defense of Tan Son Nhut.

An AC-119 Shadow gunship, which had spent the night defending the base perimeter, landed for fuel and ammunition. After refueling and rearming, the Shadow took off again. The gunship orbited the air base firing on advancing NVA troops and was soon joined by a pair of A-1s. The Skyraiders made repeated runs over NVA positions until NVA gunners downed one with an SA-7. The second A-1 pilot continued his attacks until his fuel and ordnance were used up. All the while, the AC-119 kept its fire directed on advancing enemy forces. About 7 AM the Shadow's luck ran out. Another *Strella* scored a direct hit and the AC-119 fell in flames. Three crewmen managed to bail out, but one chute became entangled in the flaming debris and carried its wearer to a flaming death.

In the final evacuation, over a hundred VNAF aircraft arrived in Thailand, including twenty-six F-5s, eight A-37s, eleven A-1s, six C-130s, thirteen C-47s, five C-7s, and three AC-119s. Additionally close to 100 VNAF helicopters landed on U.S. ships off the coast, although at least half were jettisoned. Two 0-1s managed to land on the *USS MIDWAY*, one of which was also jettisoned. On 30 May 1975, Saigon fell and all remaining South Vietnamese forces were ordered to surrender. For the VNAF thirty-five long years of war had come to an end.

THIRTEEN ABANDONED/DERELICT C-7s

Following the retreat from the Central Highlands the fighting spirit had gone out of the South Vietnamese. The important city of Da Nang fell after defense was hampered by conflicting orders and mass confusion. Da Nang airfield was also abandoned with little effort to destroy aircraft unable to evacuate. Reconnaissance photos taken after the evacuation, reveal a portion of the 180 aircraft and helicopters left behind for NVA use. (USAF via Bell)

At Xuan Loc ARVN 18th Division with VNAF support held off the NVA until overwhelmed by sheer numbers. The VNAF flew over 600 sorties during the battle for Xuan Loc, helicopters ferried in troops while F-5s and A-37s conducted air strikes. With the fall of Xuan Loc all hope of halting the NVA advance disappeared. (USAF)

(Left) After the fall of Xuan Loc there was a massive exodus of VNAF aircraft from of South Vietnam. These A-37s and U-17s are parked on the ramp at U-Tapao, Thailand after their escape. The A-37 was from the 546th FS based at Bien Thuy. (JEM Aviation)

(Below Left) A number of flyable A-1 Skyraiders were removed from storage to join the exodus. These worn A-1Es, formerly of the 23rd Tactical Wing at Bien Hoa, sit forlornly in the grass at U-Tapao Thailand after their VNAF fuselage insignia had been quickly painted out. (JEM Aviation)

U.S. officials were concerned over the fate of the newer aircraft in the VNAF inventory, such as the F-5E. Eventually twenty-two F-5Es were flown to Thailand by VNAF pilots where they were disarmed by USAF maintenance personnel at U-Tapao. (USAF)

Over 130 aircraft were flown out of South Vietnam to Thailand before the country fell. U-Tapao soon became crowded with VNAF aircraft including these F-5As, F-5Es, U-17s, and an Air Vietnam DC-3. A number of these aircraft were turned over to American allies in Asia. (USAF)

(Right) A large number of helicopters, lacking the range to fly to Thailand, chose instead to fly to the US evacuation fleet off the Vietnamese coast. There were so many that the ship's crews had to push many overboard. This final act became the scene which was imprinted on the minds of Americans as the nightly news recorded the South Vietnamese defeat. (Chenoweth)

This 0-1E made a successful deck landing on the USS Midway during OPERATION FREQUENT WIND, the first time an O-1 had ever landed on an aircraft carrier. The 0-1 was returned to the United States and eventually put on display at the Naval Air Museum in Pensacola, Florida, the only VNAF aircraft to be preserved in the U.S. (Daniels)

Appendixes

Appendix I
South Vietnamese Air Force Order of Battle, 1972

1st Air Division
41st Tactical Wing (Da Nang)
110th LS 0-1, U-17
120th LS 0-1, U-17
516th FS A-37
528th FS A-37

51st Tactical Wing (Da Nang)
213th HS UH-1
233rd HS UH-1
239th HS UH-1
427th TS C-7

4th Air Division
74th Tactical Wing (Binh Thuy)
116th LS 0-1, U-17
122nd LS 0-1, U-17
211th HS UH-1
217th HS UH-1
520th FS A-37
526th FS A-37

84th Tactical Wing (Soc Trang)
225th HS UH-1
227th HS UH-1

2nd Air Division
62nd Tactical Wing (Nha Trang)
114th LS 0-1, U-17
524th FS A-37
534th FS A-37 (at Phan Rang)

92nd Tactical Wing (Nha Trang)*
215th HS UH-1
219th HS UH-1
817th CS AC-47

Air Training Center (Nha Trang)**
12th SS 0-1, T-41

5th Air Division
33rd Tactical Wing (Tan Son Nhut)
314th SAMS C-47, U-17, UH-1, DC-6B,
  Aero Commander
415th TS C-47
716th RS RC-47, EC-47, U-6A
718th RS EC-47

53rd Tactical Wing (Tan Son Nhut)
413th TS C-119
421st TS C-123
423rd TS C-123
425th TS C-123
819th CS AC-119

3rd Air Division
23rd Tactical Wing (Bien Hoa)
112th LS 0-1, U-17
124th LS 0-1, U-17
514th FS A-1
518th FS A-1
522nd FS F5A, F5B, RF5
536th FS F5A, F5B

43rd Tactical Wing (Bien Hoa)
221st HS UH-1
223rd HS UH-1
231th HS UH-1
237th HS CH-47
245th HS UH-1

6th Air Division
72nd Tactical Wing (Pleiku)
118th LS 0-1, U-17
229th HS UH-1
235th HS UH-1
530th FS A-1

82nd Tactical Wing (Phu Cat)
241st HS CH-47
243rd HS UH-1
429th TS C-7
431st TS C-7
532nd FS A-37

* 92nd TW was probably formed from assests of 62nd, possibly in early 1973. 62nd TW would have composed of these units prior to the divison of assests.
** Not officially under 2nd Air Division, reported to VNAF Headquarters in Saigon.

Appendix II
South Vietnamese Air Force. Projected Order of Battle, After ENHANCE and ENHANCE PLUS

1st Air Division
41st Tactical Wing (Da Nang)
538th FS F5₁
550th FS A-37

51st Tactical Wing (Da Nang)
247th HS CH-47
257th HS UH-1

4th Air Divison
74th Tactical Wing (Binh Thuy)
546th FS A-37

84th Tactical Wing (Soc Trang)
249th HS CH-47
255th HS UH-1

2nd Air Division
62nd Tactical Wing (Nha Trang)
548th FS A-37 (at Phan Rang)

92nd Tactical Wing
253rd HS UH-1

Air Training Center (Nha Trang)
920 TrS T-37₂

5th Air Division
33rd Tactical Wing (Tan Son Nhut)
720th RS RC-119
821st CS AC-119

53rd Tactical Wing (Tan Son Nhut)
259th HS UH-1
435th TS C-130 ₃
437th TS C-130 ₃

3rd Air Division
23rd Tactical Wing (Bien Hoa)
536th FS F5
542nd FS F5
544th FS F5

43rd Tactical Wing
251st HS UH-1

6th Tactical Wing
72nd Tactical Wing (Pleiku)
none

82nd Tactical Wing (Phu Cat)
540th FS F5

1 These units may have been partially requipped with F5E's but this cannot be confirmed although the VNAF did receive the more advanced F5E's.
2 920th TrS and 12th SS may have been combined as one unit.
3 When the C-130 aircraft were received the various C-47, C-119, and C-123 units were deactivated. Their personnel were used to staff the two C-130 units; in addition excess personnel were used to man the newl
created F5 and A-37 units.

General Notes:
1) Cessna 0-2's were also supplied and supposedly traded on a one for one basis for 0-1's.
2) The various F5 units may have been formed into a seperate wing but this cannot be confirmed.